# A Gift That Changed The World

Stewardship In The Local Church

## By Ronald J. Kovack

*A Gift That Changed The World*
by Ron Kovack

Printed in the United States of America

ISBN 1-597810-50-9

www.xulonpress.com

# Foreword

This is a book about charitable giving, church management principles and real life examples of gifts which changed the world for millions of people. Only through the eyes of history is one able to look back, determine the proximate cause of an event and weigh the impact and historical significance. The gift of the Corinthian Church found in 2nd Corinthians 8-9 was such an event. The author examines the text and makes a stunning conclusion.

How to conduct a stewardship program and administer church funds are also discussed from the prospective of a chairman of stewardship at a growing church over a twenty year period. May God bless you and increase your faith and giving as a result of reading this book.

# Table Of Contents

# CHAPTER 1

# A Gift That Changed the World

I settled into my morning routine, reading the morning newspaper and drinking my second cup of coffee. It seemed like Tuesday, September 11, 2001 was starting out like so many days before it. September in Florida can be muggy and it appeared that it was going to be just such a day with the humidity at 100% and the temperature in the low ninety degrees. I clicked on the TV in my office and glanced at the pre-opening comments of the stock market on CNBC without paying too much attention. Suddenly, the program was interrupted and the network cut away to a breaking news story. That in itself was not unusual, for such breaks were common as the network would often go on location for such events as an Alan Greenspan speech or a presidential announcement or some other event which may affect the markets. What was unusual, however, was a picture of one of the World Trade Center buildings in the financial district of Manhattan and there was a fire in the building about three quarters up from the ground.

There was a great deal of speculation among the reporters as to the source of the fire. One announcer said there were unconfirmed reports that a small plane had crashed into the side of the building. Remembering that a B-25 crashed into the side of the Empire State Building a long time ago it certainly seemed plausible, but that was at a time when there were limited navigational aids and it occurred in the midst of a heavy fog. The screen I was looking at showed that it was a bright clear day in Manhattan.

I yelled to the rest of the people working nearby to come quickly to my office! "There's something here you have to see." Since I had the only TV close at hand, I wanted the rest of the folks to see it. The staff came to my office quickly for they seemed to sense that it was an urgent matter by the tone in my voice. As the subsequent events unfolded, pieces of the puzzle fit together and started to give a clear picture of what had just taken place right before our eyes. We were all aware of one thing: our life in the United States perhaps in the entire world just changed. Things would never be the same as it was prior to the events we had just witnessed that day.

Throughout history there have been events that at first glance seem to be insignificant in the overall scheme of things. Events which seem to be side bars of history, of little importance, yet if fully understood, they are not simply landscape for the main event but actually comprise the framework which will shape things to come. Not just a hors d'oeuvre, but the main entrée at the banquet of life. Often time history-changing events, when viewed by historians with perfect hindsight, are quite obvious in their importance. An example would be the Battle of Midway during the Second World War where the U.S. Navy won a hard-fought victory at sea against the Japanese Navy.

The battle changed the war and it was obvious to all that it was going to be the turning point of the war. By turning back the Japanese Navy, the U.S. took control of a group of islands from which air strikes could be launched against the Japanese mainland. With the United States industrial might out-producing Japan in planes and bombs, it would only be a matter of time until the Japanese were pounded into submission. The atomic bomb hastened the day and it too changed history, and it was obvious to all that it would.

Other events which change history are only understood when they are uncovered and brought to light by assembling the facts as one might fit together the pieces of a puzzle and present, as one great radio commentator would put it, "the rest of the story." An example of this is the stoning of Stephen, the first deacon, "*a man full of faith*" as we read in Acts 6:5, who preaches to the Sanhedrin (Acts chapter 7) and is stoned to death. As a result of the stoning to which the great Apostle Paul, then called Saul prior to his conversion, gave his approval (Acts Ch.8: 1), a great persecution broke out against the Church at Jerusalem and scattered the members. We read in Acts 8:4 that "*those who had been scattered preached the Word wherever they went.*" So we may conclude that as a result of Stephen's stoning, God used the event to take the gospel outside of Jerusalem using lay people. I say "lay people" because we read in verse one of Ch: 8 that *"all except the Apostles were scattered throughout Judea and Samaria."* Laymen were at the forefront of spreading the Word, the Apostles stayed home! *"Later when the Apostles heard that Samaria had accepted the Word of God, they sent Peter and John to them."* (Acts 8:14)

By assembling the pieces of various seemingly unrelated events and then standing back and looking at them through the eyes of history, we see how they are woven together to form a conclusion. A conclusion prepared by God using secondary causes to form an outcome unlike anything we expected but yet, the outcome of his perfect will and plan.

Perhaps the classic example is when Joseph's brothers sold him into slavery for twenty shekels of silver to the Ishmaelites who took him to Egypt. (Gen. 37:28) Later in his life when Joseph was the instrument by which God chose to save many lives, Joseph told his brothers: *"You intended to harm me, but God intended it for good to accomplish what is now being done, the saving of many lives."* (Gen. 50:20 NIV) With great insight, Joseph could look back at the events of his life and see God's hand in all that took place. The selling of Joseph into slavery was an event, which changed the course of history!

It is precisely the type of event, which took place in Corinth, and the thesis of this book, which is: **The "promised" gift of the Church at Corinth, as it was used by God for His glory, would in due time, change the course of history!**

Let us examine the unfolding of events in 2 Corinthians

as the Apostle Paul begins his instructions on the topic of "faith promise giving," and the gift, that the Church at Corinth had promised.

Paul opens 2 Corinthians 8 with the declaration in verse one that he wished to reveal (gnorizo) to the Corinthians, or make known to them, the grace that God had given the Macedonian churches. While not the last topic to be dealt with in the letter, it is, as usual with the topic of money, one of the last items of business to be addressed within the area of instructions for the churches.

The reasons for telling the Corinthian church what the Macedonian churches were doing in the area of stewardship may be speculated on at this point. First, would be lifting up a role model which the church could look at: that giving is not just something done as an afterthought, as a tax on the right to belong to the eternal kingdom, or something that is a part of salvation, that is, "you have to take the bad with the good." Quite the contrary, <u>giving provides the opportunity to have a part in the ministry of the donee to the extent that the donor actually participates spiritually with the donee.</u> To grasp this principle is to come to a new awareness of the blessings God bestows on a giver. The Macedonian churches obviously became aware of it as they *"entirely on their own urgently pleaded with us for the privilege of sharing in this service to the saints."*

The churches in Macedonia had the right theology and the right priority in their giving. They recognized the opportunity as being presented by God himself, whereby they could have an impact far beyond their church, their town, and their country. They recognized that the benefits of the gift, while used in this world, would have an eternal reward. Perhaps Jim Elliot said it best: "He is no fool who gives what he cannot keep to gain that which he cannot lose." Right thinking on the part of the Macedonian churches "*welled up in rich generosity* (2 Corinthians 8:2), filled them with overflowing joy so that they pleaded with the apostle that they be allowed to be reduced to the point where they were insolvent themselves. (2 Corinthians 8:4)

Can you imagine standing in the final judgment next to someone from the Macedonian church who had given as much "*as they were able and beyond their ability*" to the extent they became needy themselves? We in America, who are rich beyond the wildest dreams of the Macedonian Church are sure to be embarrassed. Yet Christians in America return to their homes after hearing a sermon on tithing much like the rich young ruler who "*went away to his home sad because he had much wealth*" (Matthew 19:22). Why is it that one church in history can give to the point of exhaustion while another continues to stuff itself like swine at an overflowing feeding trough? I believe that the answer can be found in the first verse of chapter 8, which says "*the grace that God has given*" (2 Corinthians 8:1).

Apart from God's Spirit convicting, cleansing, and changing man's "wanter" as Dr. D. James Kennedy calls it, man cannot and will not part with his physical treasure and exchange it for heavenly treasure. (Matthew 6:20). Like the treasure of the Kingdom of God, future treasure remains hidden (Matthew 13:44) to most wealthy American Christians. At a recent church service I heard a Pastor say, "This church has all the money it needs; the problem is it's still in your wallets and purses"

One can only speculate on what it will take to loosen the purse strings of Americans. I submit it will take nothing less than the Spirit of God coming upon the people of God to convict them about their lack of giving from their abundance. And yet pastors across America are reluctant to preach on the topic of money and giving. At a time in history in which the pastor is reluctant to speak out against abortion in America, which has been called the American holocaust, the topic of giving remains a far more difficult subject for most pastors. After all, they don't want to appear to have false motives for preaching and be criticized, particularly in the mega church where the member is able to cloak himself in the general success of a church that has a greater than normal ratio of giving. The traditional business axiom goes something like this: 80% of your business comes from 20% of your accounts. Giving in mega churches tends to be 95%-5% where a small percentage of the congregation gives almost 95% of the revenue.

A study by the stewardship department at one large church discovered that of all the members who joined the church during one year, 50% failed to give anything the following year; yet there they were sitting in church enjoying the blessings God has bestowed on his people. Should such a person standing on the winning side in the Great Assize find himself standing next to a member of the Macedonian church Paul is speaking about, shame and regret hardly seem adequate to describe the feeling they shall obviously feel.

Yet even more embarrassed will be the pastor of that

individual, who will be at a loss for words when the member asks the pastor: "Why didn't you teach me about these things? I attended church just about every Sunday for years, and I never heard you say anything about the blessing God bestowed on those who tithe and give from their abundance. Oh, you alluded to it once during the year in what you called the yearly stewardship sermon, but you never opened the scriptures on this topic for me." It will indeed be a sad day for many as they realize what could have been, even as the rich young ruler does today.

In defense of the pastor however, it must be recognized that the subject of money is a stumbling block to many people, particularly the non-Christian and the new or imma-ture Christian, and so the pastor is, in effect, caught on the horns of a dilemma – he's criticized if he preaches on giving but on the other hand, he feels guilty if he doesn't teach the flock about the fabulous grace of giving.

What then is the answer? How can a pastor train a congregation to give as much as they can without appearing to comprise his position as the teacher? I believe one way may be found in 2 Corinthians 8, and the answer is to allow senior leadership to develop the gift of giving face-to-face, while the pastor provides vision and oversight, just as Paul did for the churches in Macedonia and Corinth. More on this later, as we continue to look at the Macedonian church and the reasons Paul shares with the church in Corinth about the giving of the Macedonians.

Perhaps a second reason Paul used the Macedonian church's giving, as a point of information to the Corinthians was to let them be encouraged by the faith—in—action example the Macedonians provided. "Faith," the writer in Hebrews tells us, *"is being sure of what we hope for and certain of what we do not see."*(Hebrews 11:1) It is not only the *"ancients who are commended for it"* but now the Macedonians can be lifted up as demonstrating their faith by giving up that which they most cherish and cling to – for that which they could only see from a distance. (Hebrews 11:2)

The topic of money and how much one should give will always be of interest to the new believer. The reasons for this mindset will vary from person to person but the question remains the same: What does God expect of me financially now that I have become a Christian? It was no different for the Corinthians who asked the question of the Apostle Paul.

It all begins in 1 Corinthians 16 with Paul's instructions about the collection for God's people. *"Do what I told the Galatian churches to do, on the first day of the week, each one of you should set aside a sum of money in keeping with his income, saving it up so that when I come, no collections will have to be made."* (1 Corinthians 16:1-2) The gift was to be sent to Jerusalem for the saints.

In the meantime, Paul was headed through Macedonia and was staying in Ephesus. (1 Corinthians 6:5-8) Paul sent brothers to Corinth (1 Corinthians 16:12) and Titus (2 Corinthians 7:6) returned to Paul with a report on the Church (2 Corinthians 7:7 and 13). Paul said he would send the gift to Jerusalem with a letter of introduction, but he might decide to take it himself. At any rate, the giving was to be done weekly and set aside so that no collecting would be necessary when he was there with them. (Paul did, indeed, end up taking the gift to Jerusalem, a fact confirmed before Felix in Acts 24:17.) (Also see Romans 15:25–26)

# CHAPTER 2

# Giving In The Church In America Today

In his book, <u>Giving and Stewardship in an Effective Church: A Guide for Every Member,</u> Kennon L. Callahan writes, "People give generously and graciously, eagerly and cheerfully to God's mission in six major ways." [1] He calls them six "giving doors."[2] They are the following:[3]

- Spontaneous giving
- Major community worship giving
- Special planned giving
- Short-term major project giving
- Annual Budget Giving
- Enduring giving

Callahan further postulates: "...people move through distinctive stages in their giving pilgrimage as they learn to give generously." [4] He goes on to break down each "door" and explain his understanding of each as they apply to the local church. I like what he has to say about each of the "doors," for his conclusions and his theology are solid. From a church management stand point, however, I believe there is a better way to organize the concepts into a framework other than "doors." The framework I will present is not the product of my own intellectual design. I simply filled in the blanks and developed what I was given. Any congregation, or for that matter any charitable organization can do the same.

Early in my career, as an Elder in charge of Stewardship, I had the opportunity to meet and learn from one of the most knowledgeable men I ever met in the area of charitable funds management. He (is) was a pastor of an inner city Presbyterian Church in St. Louis, Missouri. A former stockbroker who was converted and called to the ministry, he brought the financial and management skills he learned on Wall Street to the pulpit. He was able to say that looking back in his life, God trained him for a special task. His name was (is) Rev. William McConkey.

He shared his approach to church financial management with me one afternoon between breaks from consulting with a locally based ministry. I took the concepts he passed on to me and adapted them to the goals and objectives of my local church in a hybrid philosophy of financial management. The genius of the concepts he shared with me is they are transferable and adaptable across a broad range of applications. As I was given them freely so I give them to you with the hope that God will use them for his glory—and change the world by making you a better manager of his funds.

Giving in the local church has three levels or segments, that require education and application by those in charge of stewardship. I use the term *stewardship* to denote the income side of the income and expense ledger of the financial statement. The expense side comes under the finance department. I am sure there are many churches where stewardship and finance are the same job function; separating them, however, has many advantages whereas responsibility for each side of the income and expense ledger is clearly identified. While I am going to relate the concepts as they apply to the local church, keep in mind the transferability to a multitude of applications. The concepts are: Entry Level, Sustaining Level, and the Developmental Level.

The Entry Level is the all-important foundation for giving in which an individual learns the what, when, where, and why of giving. It is usually one of the first topics new believers question after they come Christ. Such was the case of the Corinthian Church. Subsequent to Paul's visit to Corinth, the Church had a number of questions and situations which needed to be clarified and discussed—questions of immoral behavior, lawsuits, marriage, food sacrificed to idols, worship, spiritual gifts, the resurrection and, of course, giving.

Stewardship education is the first part of the Entry-Level segment. In 1 Corinthians 16:12 Paul instructs the church on the procedure of giving, specifically the what, when, where, and why. He writes, "Now about the collection for God's people: *Do what I told the Galatian churches to do. On the first day of every week, each one of you should set aside a sum of money in keeping with his income, saving it up so that when I come, no collections will have to be made."* (1 Corinthians 1–2). We see basic education in the entry level along with specific directions and a disclosure of how the funds will be used; the gift will be sent to Jerusalem or Paul himself will take the gift. (1Corinthians 16:4),

In case you missed it: It is what I told the Galatian churches to do. Each one set aside a sum of money. The unstated who is, of course, the Corinthians and the Galatians.

- When—on the first day of the week.
- Where—saving it up in a fund.
- Why—to give the Church at Jerusalem.
- How much to give—a sum in keeping with each individuals income.

Entry Level at the local church today is not much different than it was back in those days. Instruction in what God expects from his people is a core value to the membership process. As prospective members seek information on church membership, the topic of money is sure to arise and it is best dealt with in a proactive context. One successful way to do it is devote a class to teaching the Scriptures on the promises of God to those who are faithful in their giving. Beginning in the Old Testament with Malachi 3, the basic building block requirement of the tithe and the promises God makes will be of great interest to the new member. God's faithfulness is the key point to highlight.

The church budget amount and how it is spent is valuable information at the entry level because it not only discloses how the funds are used by the overseers, but it also stretches the vision of the people when they see how their tithes and offerings are ministering God's Word in ways they never dreamed. Furthermore, the accountability aspect of full disclosure assures a member the administration of the funds is above reproach. In a time of scandals and skepticism brought on by the uncovering of bogus schemes, of which I have seen my share, disclosure cannot be stressed enough.

At one church that has been successful in the administration of its funds, the new member is asked to fill out a pledge card estimating the amount they expect to give in the coming year. It is explained to the donor, the pledge card is not a contract and it will never be called into account with the church. It is, however, a management tool the finance committee may use when estimating the amount of ministry for the coming year. As a church budget grows larger each year, the pledge card becomes an important element of forecasting the amount of the budget. If the overseers overestimate revenues and the funds do not materialize, the church doesn't pay its bills on time, salaries and staff positions are cut, missionaries are not paid and the church witness is impugned and denigrated—definitely not a good testimony!

If, on the other hand, the church takes in more money than anticipated, the church becomes deficient in its mission because it did not realize all of the ministry God provided through the people. To have a pile of money left over at the end of the year is just as bad, maybe worse, than having a budget shortfall. Having a pledge card for management purposes is important, but is also important from the people's standpoint.

Consider the end of the chapter of Malachi 3. After listening to God's rebuke for not tithing, robbing God and hearing the grumbling, which God calls to account (Malachi 3:13-15), we read, *"Then those who feared God talked with each other, and the Lord listened and heard. A scroll of remembrance was written in his presence concerning those who feared the Lord and honored His name.* The word used for scroll in Hebrew is seper, which may also be translated letter, certificate, deed, or dispatch. The list of uses is not exhaustive; it could also mean, document.

Another way to look at this is to say that when the people heard the rebuke by the Lord for not tithing and grumbling, those who "feared the Lord" repented. They talked with each other and they put down in writing what they were going to do to correct the situation. I would like to think they filled out a pledge card, but of course, there is no warrant for such speculation. However, a document to bring to mind the conclusion they reached regarding the tithe and offerings and the harsh things they said was drafted and executed. It is very interesting to see God's reaction to the document and the discussion. He says, *"They will be mine." "In the day when I make up my treasured possession, I will spare them just as in compassion a man spares his son who serves him"* (Malachi 3:17). It is as though God is saying you made up your use of possessions list and I will make up my treasured possessions. God is certainly talking about Judgment Day, and He says, *"And you will again see the distinction between the righteous and the wicked, between those who serve God and those who do not"* (Malachi 3:17).

Certainly there is a division between givers and non-givers, a subject I will talk more about later in this book. In the educational element of the entry level, a point that should be reiterated is that God doesn't need a member's money. God declares, *"For every animal of the forest is mine and the cattle on a thousand hills"* (Psalm 50:10). *Further, "The world is mine and all that is in it"* (Psalm 50:12b). Our giving is only giving back to him, what he has given to us—to the praise of His glory.

The second level of church stewardship, the <u>Sustaining Level</u>, is a lot like caring for a garden that is growing and producing a crop. The idea is to feed it, weed it and care for it, harvesting the future crop it will provide. In a similar fashion, the sustaining level is the annual renewal of giving commitments of tithes and offerings. I have often wrestled with the amount of effort and the type of direction that should be devoted to the sustaining level.

There is a tension between what is in good taste and what is not. For example, a visitor walks into the church for the very first time and it happens to be Stewardship Sunday, when the pastor preaches a sermon on tithes and offerings—money.

The visitor goes away and later that week, someone learns the visitor attended church and asks, "How did you like the service?"

The visitor responds to the inquiry by saying, "Well, not much has changed. All the preacher talked about was money."

If, on the other hand the pastor frames the message and tells the people: "This is Stewardship Sunday, and it is the one Sunday a year I teach on the topic of tithing and gifting—money." It just so happens that the visitor chose that particular Sunday to visit the church and it is quite clear to me that God sent the visitor to the church because he wanted to teach the visitor about the grace of giving.

If the visitor comes to church four Sundays in a row and hears a sermon on giving, it is not only the visitor who will be turned off, but also most of the church. So there is the tension. Preach about money too much or not preach and teach about it at all during the year.

Not to preach and teach on the topic of money in the sustaining level is to leave out an important element in the renewal process. Coming back to the garden metaphor, it's like planting the garden, but then abandoning it by not caring for it. God's people need to be reminded of the blessings God wants to bestow on those who are faithful in their stewardship. Faithful—full of faith. A definition of the Greek word for faith (Pistis) that I like is this: "A persuasion which is not the outcome of imagination, but which is based on fact". The sustaining level reminds us of the fact of God's promises and His faithfulness.

How each church goes about the annual renewal is for the most part a judgment call by the leadership of the church. I say that because each church is distinctive in its demographics. Whatever form the annual event takes, it should be done in a manner appropriate for the demographics, in proper balance and in good taste.

Some of the elements of the sustaining level can be:

- Testimonies at the worship service,
- Pledge cards inserted in the Sunday bulletin that

remind the people of the church's need to be accurate in forecasting revenues for ministry in the coming year.

- Posters of Scripture verses relating to God's promises displayed in prominent places such as Sunday School and hallways.
- Pamphlets on the topic of tithing enclosed with a church mailing.
- Sunday school classes devoted to the topic of giving.
- Scripture memory verses on cards, bookmarks, and, of course,
- An annual stewardship sermon from the pulpit.

These are but some of the things a church can do to tend the garden God has planted, as He graciously allows people to have a part in the work that He is doing.

The third level of church stewardship, the <u>Developmental Level</u>, is an open ended and creative level that goes beyond regular giving and enters into an aspect of giving that incorporates faith and trust.

If Entry Level and Sustaining Level may be likened to high school and college, the Development Level is the graduate school of giving. The first two levels are based on obedience and faithfulness in giving on the part of people as they learn what is required of them by God.

The third level, however, throws gasoline on the fire of God's promises to those who by faith give out of the abundance God provides. It is the high standard of giving set forth in the New Testament that we have discussed earlier.

Furthermore**, I believe it is in the best interest of the people for the leadership of the local church to present opportunities for giving above and beyond the tithe.** I say this because the people will be blessed by God as they stretch their faith and give in love as the Father has given. (Not that there is any comparison whatsoever of his Gift to us in his Son).

In his book <u>Generous Living</u>, Ron Blue breaks down an individuals giving as: "Should Give, Could Give, and Would Give."[5] He makes a really good point. "How much you give is not so much a reflection of your wealth as it is of your relationship with God. Any time you sacrifice something in order to give—be it money possession, time, or something else—you are giving at the 'could give' level"[6]

"Would Give," on the other hand is pre-committed faith giving and results in a life of faith and joy. Blue's categories of individual giving differentiate between giving above and beyond the tithe from gifting out of an abundance God has provided. Blue writes about individual responsibility, while I deal more with church administration in conjunction with individual giving.

It is my belief that church members are "raised" in their level of giving by the leadership of the local church and the way it happens is the same way it is always happened; by having their vision stretched. It occurs when church members see and hear what God is doing and they have a desire to have a part in it, by faith. We read, *"This is what the ancients were commended for"* (Hebrews 11:2). *They were all commended "yet none of them received what had been promised." God had planned something better for us so that only together with us would they be made perfect"* (Hebrews 11:39-40).

We know when we give in this world to the cause of Christ we don't expect anything in return, but see a reward only from a distance. That is the way it should be, yet I believe giving activates the power of God in the life of the church as well as in the life of the individual donor.

The Developmental Level provides projects, special requests, particular ministry opportunities as well as capital projects as opportunities for giving.

A second part of the Developmental Level is planned giving, or deferred giving, that incorporates such things as testamentary giving through wills, estates, trusts, and bequests. I will deal with the topic of developmental giving later in this book and will discuss specific types of gifts and transfers in planned giving. For now, however, I will like to discuss opportunities in current giving at the local church that are typical examples of this level of giving.

A special project that is an appropriate investment of funds is a short term missions trips to a third world country, especially if the church youth are the ones going under the leadership of church staff. The annual missions conference, Gideon Sunday, a school funds drive, are just a few of the examples of the kinds of developmental projects that raise the giving level of a church. From the Deacon's benevolent fund to a local food pantry supply drive, developmental giving raises the spiritual temperature of the local church as well as that of its members.

Outreach to the local community, especially to the poor, is always a project near to the heart of God. You may recall helping the poor was the occasion of Peter the Apostle being sent to Tabitha/Dorcas after she died because she was one who was always "doing good and helping the poor" (Acts 9:36). There are many references to helping the poor; and some form of help, either directly with cash or food or indirectly with a thrift store, or similar outlet are very worthwhile projects.

The bottom line is a church becomes a "giving church" the same way an individual does: *"be transformed by the renewing of your mind, then you will be able to test and approve what God's will is, His good, pleasing and perfect will"* (Romans 12:2).

When the local church renews its mindset, the whole community as well as the church begins to change. I know a local church whose impact is felt worldwide because of its faithful giving. Only in eternity will the perfect will of God illumine those gifts for all to see.

The chests of the treasure "stored up" according to Matthew 5:20 will be opened to the glory of God. Will your church have one to open? What about you individually? What is the system of financial management in operation at your local church?

# CHAPTER 3

# The Status of the Church at Corinth

The city of Corinth was positioned as a hub of commerce and influence. Located on an important strait between Athens to the east and Italy to the west, it was a port city near the center of a circle comprised of the Sea of Adria on the west, which borders the east coast of Italy; the Mediterranean Sea to the south; and the Aegean Sea to the east, which joins the Black Sea to the northeast. It had an international cosmopolitan atmosphere about it, much like a Miami or New York in today's America. Paul, in his own inimitable way, being used by God, had made a good beginning there among some local businessmen and women.

Perhaps it was through Priscilla and Aquila who Paul says risked their lives for him (Romans 16:4), or other prominent citizens. The Church did have as members Erastus, the city's director of public works, and Gaius, who was probably at least moderately wealthy.

It is when the local businessmen catch fire for the Lord that things can really start to happen in a local church. It seems they bring all the gifts God has given to them and the skills they have honed, and put them to use in the church. Moreover, they provide a level of leadership which models for others. Other peers follow, and soon the church has a base of good support of financial and spiritual commitment and strength.

The downside is, sometimes they bring an attitude and brashness they used in the business world, which has no part in the body of Christ. Praise God who by his Spirit does not stop with the act of salvation, but continues to shape and polish lives as he makes them become more godly through the process known as sanctification. It certainly tended to be the case for the Church at Corinth because, having received Paul's first letter, they reacted with godly sorrow. I can almost hear the businessmen of the church as they gathered to consider the instructions in 1 Corinthians 16 regarding the poor in Jerusalem. "Let's put together a package that will really take care of those people." While I realize such a statement is pure conjecture on my part, I can assure you it is exactly what would have occurred at my church. I have seen it happen time and time again as a cause comes before our body and moves our hearts to action. A missionary with a special need, an opportunity to feed the poor or homeless, or just the regular drive to annually fund a missionary campaign above and beyond the regular line item of the budget, will have good success.

Would the Church at Corinth, with its probable affluence,

have been less than my church or yours? Probably not! Such a capital campaign does, however, take some time to put together. Some major gifts, along with the general fund-raising, would certainly need to take place. A similar situation of gifts in kind would be further aggravated in an economy that dealt in the trading of goods and less in services. In such a fund-raising event there would be all kinds of items pledged. (I know of one local campaign where a bull was donated and brought to the church). Consider our early American culture where a doctor was often paid with things like pigs, chickens, and fresh eggs when they made house calls.

It's easy to understand why preachers and commentators have never quite grasped what is going on here in this eighth and ninth chapter of 2 Corinthians because they never had to deal with "gifts in kind." Most of the time these are left for others to manage for the pastor. As Chairman of the Stewardship Committee at my church for fifteen years, it has been the job of the committee, for the most part, to deal with these types of gifts.

Paul hears about the status of the Corinthian Church when the brothers return with a report. (2 Corinthians 7:6). He is particularly encouraged by the way that the church dealt with the sinful brother, the willingness of the church to give above and beyond their normal giving, and the promise they made about a gift in the future, a faith promise pledge. I will devote more time to that faith promise pledge in as much as it is the theme of this book; but first I want to look at four ways God used the Corinthian report in the life of Paul to comfort and encourage him.

The first way was by the safe return of Titus himself.

While we take safe travel for granted today, it wasn't always the case in Paul's day. Robbers and thugs were the norm as they lay in wait for passing prey in the countryside. No local police, no phones to call for help. Travelers had to defend themselves, particularly in isolated stretches between towns. To combat this, men armed themselves with swords and traveled with companions. (You may recall the victim of the Good Samaritan's ministry wasn't so fortunate. In teaching the parable Jesus used an example that the people clearly understood, as he did in all the parables.)

The second comfort to Paul was the fact that the Corinthians treated Titus well. Having been the messenger of such a strong letter to the church, Titus could have delivered it and then have become the object of resistance by those it affected. Less than the best of care, a "freeze out," or a general cold shoulder were some of the possibilities of how the church could have reacted, but that wasn't the case (2 Corinthians 7:7) Titus' spirit was refreshed by all the church (2 Corinthians 7:13).

Paul was relieved that what he had said about Titus to the church and what he had told Titus about the church were both proven correct. The church at Corinth apparently fell in love with Titus and he with them, for they received him with *"fear and trembling"* and they were all obedient. No wonder when Paul asked Titus to return to Corinth with two other brothers and see to it that the faith promise pledge was completed, he was ready and willing to do it (2 Corinthians 8:6 and 8:17) with much enthusiasm.

What a logical choice by Paul to send Titus back to Corinth. Titus knew the people, they treated him well, and he probably made some close friends of church members. Had he not been treated well the first time, we may presume he would not be as anxious to return. It was the mission of Titus' return that piqued my curiosity and prompted an examination of why he returned with such highly esteemed companions. More about this issue later.

The third reason for Paul's comfort was how well the church reacted to his stern letter. After all, this was the crux of the matter, i.e., what would the Corinthians do when they received such instruction? As it turned out, the church's reaction could not have been more positive, for they had sorrow and a hurt which only God's Spirit can produce, as he convicts of sin. Godly sorrow prompted the church to repent and they had an eagerness to set things straight. In short, the letter proved to be a wake-up call to the church – something that was long overdue.

The thing about sin, which is the scariest, is that it leads to more sin of the same type; like a snowball rolling down a hill of wet snow, it gets bigger all the time. Yet when repentance comes, it has a godly sorrow with it and leads to salvation, compared to a worldly sorrow, which brings death.

Perhaps the two best examples of these kinds of sorrow are Peter and Judas. After denying the Lord three times and hearing the cock crow, which the Lord had said would happen, Peter went out and wept bitterly (Luke 22:36). Peter's sorrow was one of repentance; he confessed his sin, and Christ restored him on the beach when he asked Peter three times, *"Do you love me?"* What a good feeling it is to repent, be restored to fellowship, and once again taste of God's Spirit in your life.

Compare that with Judas' reaction, for Judas also experienced sorrow. After returning the blood money he received for betraying his Lord, he despaired, went out and hanged himself. Judas also confessed his sins (Matthew 27:4) and was seized with remorse, but it was not a sorrow that led to salvation. This is indeed a great lesson in the theological understanding of the nature of true versus false repentance

In the case of the Corinthian church, they called the sinful brother who was leading a scandalous sinful life to account, and that was the right reaction to sorrow. As a result, the sinful brother was later restored and the church learned an important lesson.

The fourth area of comfort to Paul was the love and concern the Corinthian Church still had for him in spite of the "stern" letter he had written them. (2 Corinthians 7:7, 13). Paul knew he had wounded them with his letter, yet he also knew that the church needed to hear the things he said to them. The easy way for Paul would have been to sugar coat the rebuke and intimate rather than say the things, which needed to be said. Yet having said it, Paul could not help but wonder what the reaction of the church would be toward him. Perhaps, he may have wondered, would the church act like a two-year old, pout, and get upset. Titus told him that his fears were groundless – the church had a longing for Paul, that their sorrow was deep, and they still had a fervent affection for him. Titus' report was a cause for great joy and encouragement.

If only preachers in America could take a lesson from Paul and confront America's churches with what needs to be said. The Scripture says that in the last days preachers will come and tickle the ears of the people. Rather than afflicting the comfortable, lukewarm, uninvolved church members who have allowed American morals to decline, preachers have become timid in America. They are afraid to speak out against the issues of homosexuality, abortion, and the systematic removal of God from our society, such as school prayer and all the other issues, which come under the banner of "separation of church and state."

America's preachers, for the most part, are willing to hide behind a pietistic cloak of noninvolvement, afraid of what people might say if they speak the truth and call abortion the American Holocaust and homosexuality a despicable sin. Praise God that there are preachers in America, such as Dr. D. James Kennedy, who are willing to speak out, but we need 10,000 more like him – not just a few.

What would happen in America if only 10,000 preachers started speaking out on cultural moral issues instead of preaching feel-good social gospel messages? Why Americans would rise up and demand action, repent of sin, and humble themselves before the God of our founding fathers. It would start a revival, which would sweep our land unlike any other revival before in the history of our country. Paul knew how to do it – preach it, let the chips fall where they may. (I must say, however, the signs of revival are blooming and I am greatly encouraged about what I see happening across America.)

Perhaps a reason Paul shared with the Corinthians what the Macedonians were doing was to drive home the point Dr. Phillip E. Hughes makes in his commentary The Second Epistle To the Corinthians:[7] Hughes writes "The example of the Macedonians is a practical proof that true generosity is not the prerogative of those who enjoy an adequacy of means; the most genuine liberality is frequently displayed by those who have the least to give. Christian giving is estimated in terms not of quantity, but of sacrifice." Dr. Hughes is right on target.

When a person fully understands what God requires us to give and then sees the opportunity to rise to a higher level by gifting out of the abundance, that has been provided by his Grace, a person's view of possessions changes. Instead of viewing money as a means to happiness, the mind set changes to money as a view toward ministry.

We sometimes think that nobody is supposed to know what is going on in the area of personal giving. There is a preconceived idea that it is nobody's business but the donor's, but that wasn't always the case. Now to be sure, we don't post the giving records in the church – I once belonged to a church that did – but there were special events of public giving in the Bible, such as we read in Ezra: *"When the people returned to Jerusalem, some of the heads of the families gave freewill offerings toward the rebuilding of the house o f God on its site. According to their ability they gave." (Ezra 2:68-69).*

Even before that, at the building of the tabernacle in the wilderness, in assembling the materials for building, the people brought freewill offerings for the work Moses commanded them to do. All of the giving was done in public *"and everyone who was willing and whose heart moved him came and brought an offering to the Lord."* (Exodus 36:20). We read a little later that the people had to be restrained from bringing more because they already had more than enough to do all the work (Exodus 36:6-7).

In each of these examples in the Old Testament there are several common elements of major fund-raising campaigns. The first thing that can be seen is that not everyone gives. It is clear that while the majority gives, there will always be a number of people who will not give anything. There is the 80-20 I discussed before, but I think the rule probably is more like 90-10 in most churches where 90% of the income comes from 10% of the donors. If you include large one- time gifts made outright in churches, it probably increases to 95%-5%. Let me make it clear that I have no broad base of statistical research to support these numbers, only conclusions I have made based on experience and discussion with pastors and key person- nel from a number of churches around the country, albeit a limited study

The second element is that the giving request is communicated to God's people by the leadership of the church, and it states the need- as in each of the special fund-raising appeals in Scripture. The leadership communi- cated to the people the objective and gave the people the vision for ministry. If a special project fund-raising appeal is to be made in our churches today, the people need details of the project so they can gain a vision of the ministry that will result.

Whether it is a building project using an extended capi- tal campaign or a faith promise for funding additional or current missionaries, the requests should have the specifics of who, what, when, where, and how much, in order to set clear goals for the objective. It is in such a context that God's Spirit will begin to motivate the heart of the donor to give. It is not unlike the content of the Gospel being shared with a person who then makes a decision, motivated by the Holy Spirit, unto salvation. Here is a story that illustrates the point very well.

At a critical time in the life of one particular church, there was a large amount of debt coming due for mortgage bonds, which had been issued to build the initial sanctuary on the church property. The bonds were due to mature soon and the redemption loomed like a freight train on the horizon with the congregation standing on the tracks. The image grew larger! They simply didn't have the money to pay the principal of the bonds, which were maturing. All they had been paying was the interest and some money into a sinking fund, which was going to be short. About one million dollars short! For the church it was a huge amount of money.

When the Stewardship Committee met, the idea was presented that they should attempt to retire the bonds with a surge – a special Sunday offering in the amount of the debt due, which was approximately one million dollars. While the idea seemed bizarre at first, the more they thought about it, the more plausible it became. After all, they thought, doesn't God own it all? Isn't he in control of everything? Would we be presumptuous to think that he should do that kind of fund-raising for us? Of course not! *"Ask and it will be given to you"* (Matthew 7:7); *"Ye have not because ye ask not,"* the Scriptures tell us. They asked themselves, "Are we people of faith or not?" They called the project "Million

Dollar Sunday."

As they formulated plans, set timetables, and began to assign the duties, that were needed, they realized if God wasn't in the project they were doomed to failure. So one of the first things they did was form a sub-committee to begin with prayer. The committee selected a godly old gentleman by the name of Hugh Reed and told him he had the most important committee assignment: He should enlist a large number of church members to pray and ask God to move upon the hearts of the congregation to raise the funds. Hugh has long since gone to be with the Lord but he did his job well. He had a large group praying and even went 'round the clock" as "Million dollar Sunday" approached.

To put the event into perspective: What they were attempting to do was to raise approximately 50% of their entire annual budget in one day. The criteria were either cash or a pledge, which would be paid within ninety days of the commitment day. God's Spirit did move upon the hearts of the people and the results were stunning, especially the way it happened. When "Million Dollar Sunday" arrived, the ushers collected the special envelopes and cards, which were part of the promotional activities, activities heralding the event. They had raised about 70% of the funds needed prior to the commitment day by having small group lunches at a nearby restaurant with the Pastor, the Stewardship Chairman, and the Director of Development of the church, who had recently come on staff. They just let the Pastor speak after lunch with the topic, "Where we were, where we are, and where we are going."

It seemed like they were going to fall quite short of the

goal because all of the large donors had been solicited and they still did not have all the funds needed. Then an amazing thing happened for which they were not prepared: People started giving "gifts in kind" at the collection! Diamond rings, guns, real estate, gold pieces, and all sorts of "gifts in kind." The people made sacrificial gifts because God had moved on their hearts. God received the glory because God's people had prayed and asked him to do his work among them.

There were special counting teams and extra security guards that day at the church, and distinctly remembered is the gift, which put the project over the top of the goal. It was an interest in an oil well located in the southwestern part of the United States and it was owned by a couple one would never have thought of as having any money. By the time they had valued the in-kind gifts, such as stocks, bonds and the oil well, they were over $1 million by thousands. The Church learned a very valuable lesson – a large part of a capital campaign contribution would come not in cash, but with in-kind gifts. That lesson would be put to good use in the future. It would also give me a reason to write this book.

# CHAPTER 4

# Why A Person Gives To God

W hat makes a person want to give of their money, their possessions, their time and talent? We read in 2 Corinthians 8:4, "They urgently pleaded with us for the privilege of sharing in this service to the saints." To be reduced to the point where they were actually in need themselves was the urgency of the Macedonian plea. What they deeply desired was to share what little they had with the Church in Jerusalem. As I pondered the request of the Macedonians, I could not help but ask myself "what were they thinking." Why would they have such passion about a church so far away and people they never met? What am I missing?" "*Out of the most severe trial," "extreme poverty*" and "*beyond their ability*" were the launch points for their desire to give.

I believe there are two basic reasons for such an attitude. The first is gratitude. An example is found in the account of the anointing of Jesus by the sinful woman, which is found in Luke 7:36–50. We read, *"When a woman who had led a sinful life in that town learned that Jesus was eating at the Pharisee's house, she brought an alabaster jar of perfume, and as she stood behind him at his feet weeping, she began to wet his feet with her tears. Then she wiped them with her hair, kissed them and poured perfume on them"* (Luke 7:37-38).

Knowing what was in the heart of the Pharisee Simon who was his host, Jesus poses to him the hypothetical situation of two men who owed money to a moneylender. One owed a large sum, five hundred denarii, and the other owed a relatively modest sum, fifty denarii. When neither man could pay the moneylender, the lender cancelled the debts of both men. Jesus then poses the question to Simon, *"Which of the two men will love him more?"* Simon answers Jesus correctly and says, *"I suppose the one who had the biggest debt cancelled."* Jesus then acknowledged the correct answer, *"You have judged correctly,"* He said to Simon. Jesus defends the action of the woman to Simon and then turns to the woman and says those wonderful words; *"Your sins are forgiven"* (Luke 7:48).

Here was a woman who was known to the people of the town as one who lived a sinful life. It doesn't take much imagination to figure out what was going on in the woman's life. Her reputation preceded her. The Pharisee who was hosting the dinner party certainly knew. Almost lost in the narrative is the fact that the woman brought an alabaster jar of perfume and poured it onto Jesus feet. The perfume probably represented a large part of the woman's wealth, perhaps a part of her retirement plan, yet she willingly gave it up out of gratitude.

Very little is known about the perfume, but in a similar passage found in John 12, where Mary, sister of Lazarus and Martha, pours perfume on Jesus' feet and wipes it with her hair. Judas, the bag- thief declares the perfume used *"was worth a year's wages."* While quantity and quality of the sinful woman's perfume in Luke 7 is unknown, it did represent a valuable asset— one that could be bartered for other goods in the future. Yet, the woman does not hesitate to give it out of gratitude.

Alfred Edersheim, in his book, The Life and Times of Jesus the Messiah,[8] gives us insight into the perfume as he speculates on the origin of the mixture. He writes, "We have evidence that perfumed oils—notably oil of roses and of the iris plant, but chiefly the mixture known in antiquity as "foliatum" —were largely manufactured and used in Palestine. "A flask containing perfume was worn by women around the neck and hung down below the breast. The flask containing "polyeton" (evidently the foliatum of Pliny) was used both to sweeten the breath and perfume the person. Edersheim concludes by saying, "Hence it seems at least not unlikely that the alabastron which she brought was none other than the flask of foliatum so common among Jewish women."[9] Her repentant heart, filled with gratitude, created a desire "to give that which she could not keep to gain that which she would not lose."

Lest we become confused and think for one minute that a person is saved by confession and a contrite heart, the Lord immediately cleared that up and said, "Your faith has saved you; go in peace." The verb used in the original language is in the perfect tense, active voice, and indicative mood, which is to say that the perfect tense is used to state a completed action with abiding results, i.e., the current state of affairs, which will have sustained consequences. An active voice in the text shows the one speaking carries out the action. The indicative mood is the mood of assertion and is used here to make a declaration. So what we have then is: Jesus is making the statement that the woman should go with the peace of God, knowing the exercise of her faith has resulted in an event (saved) which is a lasting event and the speaker (Jesus) strongly asserts it will happen.

With all the guilt and shame lifted from her, the woman must have left the dinner walking on a cloud. She also heard Jesus tell Simon, the host, her many, many sins have been forgiven. You just know she walked out of the dinner party with her head up, for she knew she was right with the Lord of Glory. She loved much, and she was grateful. Her gift of perfume was a gift of gratitude.

In addition to gratitude, a second reason for wanting to give is the desire to share in the work the Lord is doing—a desire to have an ownership interest in the building of the Kingdom. When a person comes to Christ, their eyes are opened and they understand the eternal consequences of giving.

Consider carefully now what Paul writes in 2 Corinthians 8:6: "*So we urged Titus since he had earlier made a begin-ning to bring also to completion this act of grace on your part.*" The word used for "bring" and "completion" is the same word (epiteleo), which is made up from the word epi, an intensive and teleo, which means, "fully achieve a goal or accomplish a purpose. It does not carry the import of improving or completing it as though it were deficient, but carries the thought of performance or accomplishment, i.e., complete with the intensive. The reason it is important is because some commentators believe that Titus and the two brothers were sent on ahead because the church was deficient in the giving instructions that Paul gave in 1 Corinthians 16:1-2. Having instructed the Corinthians to set aside their money on the first day of the week, Paul did not want to have collections made on his arrival because of the appearance it may have created—not good. The same word, "epiteleo" is used again in 2 Corinthians 8:11 and is translated "finish."

Giving God what is rightfully His can hardly be called an "act of grace": "*Will a man rob God?*" (Malachi 3:8). No, I submit Paul is talking about something entirely different here. I believe Paul is talking about liquidating gifts "in kind" – gifts that were received as part of a **Faith Promise Pledge** made by the Corinthian church. I will expound on this in the chapters ahead. The promise pledge is the subject of 2 Corinthians, chapters eight and nine. Moreover, I will show: **the faith promise pledge of the Corinthians changed the world we live in, even to this very day. <u>It was a gift that changed the world</u>**.

# CHAPTER 5

# James and His Gold Coins

Perhaps my most memorable occasion of such a gift was a gold coin collection, which had been put together by an elderly man over his lifetime. James lived a modest lifestyle, was single all his life, and lived with his elderly widowed sister. To the best of my knowledge he and his sister, a retired artist, never spent a lot of money, even drove old cars, that they regularly fixed up. The man had collected gold coins as a hobby, mostly to identify dates in history. He would recall a specific event that occurred by buying a U.S. gold coin. He purchased only the best specimen he could locate, of the most rare coin of that year. He stored his collection in a safety deposit box at the local bank where he maintained a checking account. Every once in a while he would go down to the bank, get his collection out and visit with them. Then one day his sister attended a church service at our church.

His sister had the same nominal Christian background

as James did, neither knew the Lord as their Savior but his sister came to Christ soon after her visit, and in spite of her age, close to eighty, she was really on fire for the Lord. She turned out to be quite a character and had a great mind for memorizing Scripture and preaching repentance to anyone who would listen, whether they wanted to hear it or not. Of course, this included her little brother (age 76) who lived with her. In a nutshell, she absolutely terrorized him with her three-word homily – "turn or burn." I can only imagine what he did to escape his older sister, who had suddenly become an evangelist whose calling was to get her brother saved. James, a confirmed bachelor, had women all his life trying to drag him down a church aisle, and with nowhere to run and hide, here was his sister dragging him off to church, where they actually take up collections.

To say that James lived a modest lifestyle isn't quite accurate. He was a tightwad that redefined the term for me. For example, he had only two pairs of pants, one for summer and one for winter. He never wore the summer in the winter or vice versa, but washed the pair he was wearing only when they were so soiled even he couldn't stand them. He also had two shirts, two ties, and one pair of shoes that he wore, along with one sport coat. Everything except the ties was the same color – gray with varying degrees of shade, i.e., the shirts were a little lighter than the pants and the coat almost matched the pants...making it a suit. The ties were muted multi-color specimens of the type that remain on the garage sale card tables – even after being marked down to twenty-five cents. I could only guess at James' underwear and sock supply, because I cold never bring myself to ask about it.

He lived on his Social Security check by giving his sister money to buy enough food for one meal a day – for himself. He never gave his sister any money for rent, utilities, or taxes. She owned the house outright and had some money her husband had left her, as well as some her sister who had lived with them for awhile, had left her. With the dividends on a few stocks, interest on CDs, and her Social Security check, she was able to make ends meet quite well, but with little excess or discretionary funds.

It seemed all was well for James as the years rolled by, but now his applecart was being upset because his sister got converted. Like his sister, James had a good mind and was a very engaging personality. He had a unique ability to ask a question of you, pick up on your answer, and spellbind you with a tale wrapped around your answer, mixing history or current news events and making you feel like you must have the wisdom of Solomon to give such a good answer to his question. Having mastered the art of social conversation, visits with James would slip by quickly for his visitor.

It was just about this time in the life of our church that the church school began a capital campaign to build a gymnasium, that it sorely needed. With classes K-12 and the enrollment approaching 1,000 students, the school had a wonderful academic reputation and was gaining in stature with its athletic programs as well. In addition, classrooms were maxed out with students, and additional classroom space was needed to fill the ever-increasing demand. Each year our church continued to grow and parents became more determined to avoid the public schools in south Florida for a variety of reasons, and to give their children a Christian education. While there are a number of fine public schools in south Florida, it is not the easiest place to raise children. The capital campaign drive for the school quickly reached the ears of one who would become its champion – you guessed it – James' sister.

Perhaps it is because James' sister never had any children, nor did her brother or her sister, that she was prompted to take up the cause of the school expansion. But like everything else she did with the joy of the Lord, she gave of herself and a small amount of cash first, and then turned her guns on James. As I reflect on her character, it was a lot like the Macedonians Paul writes about in 2 Corinthians 8.

For James, however, it was an entirely different matter. He had a will which left everything to his older sister, but the effectiveness of that testamentary concept had long since passed, now that they were both at an age where the lights would soon go out – at least temporarily. His sister was, of course, aware of James' gold coin collection, but could only guess at its value.

James' father had been a country doctor in Topeka, Kansas where James and his two sisters were raised. As he made his rounds visiting patients, James' dad would often have James go along with him. Not everyone paid with chickens and pigs, but wealthy patients often paid their bills with a gold coin or two. James' father would put them in a little velvet bag with a drawstring closer and give them to James, who carefully put them aside and treasured them. The family was quite prominent in Topeka and his father earned a good living practicing medicine. All of the siblings, including James, went to college and graduated.

One day, while accompanying his father, James and his dad were walking down the street together when his father had a heart attack, slumped to the street and died in James' arms. As he recounted his dad's death to me, now even as an old man in his seventies, he seemed to choke back the memory of that day. I could only imagine the scar that left on James as a young man. No wonder he cherished the gold coins so much; they were the last link to the father he loved so much.

His older, newly-turned-evangelist-fund-raiser sister had a different opinion, however, of James' gold coin collection. With no family, no heirs and estate tax rates at 70% (in those days) plus probate expense shrinkage; the only one that was going to enjoy James' gold coin collection was the U.S. government. While James and his sister did agree on that point, James was more than a little reluctant to part with his coins. I can only guess at the discussions that took place as James' sister tried to talk him into giving his collection to the church for use in building the much-needed school gymnasium. Her position, which had some validity, was that he was able to build up his collection at her expense because she paid for his living expenses all those years while he used his funds to acquire coins. Finally, she took out the big hammer: If he didn't want to donate his collection, he could find himself another place to live. James surrendered.

James' sister called me at my brokerage office one day and asked if she could stop by with her brother to talk about gifting and selling a coin collection. I set up a time to meet with them the next day, and in she came, brother in tow. As a Certified Financial Planner with tax expertise, I know that selling the coins outright, paying capital gains tax, and then giving the funds to the church wasn't the best idea. Instead, I suggested a transfer, called a charitable gift annuity whereby the donor would gift the asset to the church, and the church would give the donor and sister an income, guaranteed for the rest of their lives. The amount they agreed on was $2000 a month payable to James, and in the event he predeceased his sister, it would be payable to her for the rest of her life.

James was ecstatic with the plan. He figured his coins were going on a one-way trip, with nothing in return. James had already contacted a large coin dealer he had dealt with over the years, met with them, and asked them to take possession of his collection in anticipation of their disposition that he would advise. When I asked James to see the receipt for the collection to see what kind of pieces he had, I was shocked to see many hundreds of items listed on plain legal size paper and signed as receipt by the Dealer, a Mr. Arthur Kagin of Kagin's Numismatic Dealers. James assured me that this is how the coin business worked, and that he had known Art Kagin for over thirty years. He had many dealings with Kagins and trusted them. They were located in Des Moines, Iowa. When I later talked with Art Kagin, I found out James was correct; both Art and his son Don turned out to be gracious, honorable, honest men.

I prepared the gift annuity documents as the representative of the church and arranged a meeting with Dr. D. James Kennedy, the pastor, to execute the agreement. James showed up with his sister and signed over the collection, while Dr. Kennedy signed the annuity on behalf of the church. As we sat around and mused over the occasion, Dr. Kennedy asked James the now world-famous two questions. James knew that Heaven could not be purchased even with a gold coin collection, and when Dr. Kennedy lovingly and gently showed what Christ had done on the cross for us that we may tread the streets paved with gold, James prayed to receive Christ as his Savior. James' sister could hardly contain herself. The church had agreed that since I "had earlier made a beginning," I should "bring to completion this act of grace." Doesn't this sound just like the instructions Paul gave to Titus regarding the gift of the Corinthians? (2 Corinthians 8:6). It is God's way that once he starts using a person to bring about the goals and events he wants to happen, "There is none that can stay His hand, or say to him what doest thou." I experienced it firsthand without really knowing all about his ways in that regard.

Kagins turned out to be the right choice of dealer to liquidate the collection, a "gift in kind." They arranged a sale in the form of an auction, to be conducted at the Great Eastern Numismatic Association convention at the Americana Hotel in New York City. I attended the auction, held September 29, 30, 1978. People and dealers from all over the United States attended and there was a lot of interest in the collection that was the centerpiece of the convention auction. Kagin had done a fine job of promoting the collection and preparing a book catalogue with color pictures of some of the more important pieces. The auction was titled with James' name and called the "Church Collection."

It was the golden anniversary of the Great Eastern

Numismatic Association (1928-1978). It was also another important date in the history of the Church, the New York Bible Society's dedication of the New International Version of the Bible. They completed the new translation, and it was now being dedicated at a dinner at the Americana Hotel at the same time as the auction.

I was standing in line to register at the hotel when I noticed an Ichthus pin on an elderly gentleman standing behind me in line. I turned to him and said, "That's a pretty nice pin you are wearing." "Are you a Christian?" he responded.

I said yes, I had been one for almost three years and I had come to Christ as a result of the Evangelism Explosion program at my church. His name was Dr. Laird Harris, and he was a seminary professor. He was in town for the dedication of the NIV Bible. It turned out he had translated part of the Old Testament Hebrew into English for use in the NIV. In spite of the huge gap in spirituality between us, we hit it off and we had coffee at a hotel shop later. He found the coin collection fascinating and I was in awe of him as he related how he had memorized part of the Psalms in Hebrew on the plane to New York. I attended the dedication dinner as his guest, and as I thought about it years later, it was just as though the Lord threw that in as a little side of dessert for the occasion.

James was invited to attend the auction as a guest of the church and again as a guest of the auctioneer, but he declined, citing poor health and bad eyesight. While they were reasonably good excuses, I wondered if perhaps it wasn't that he couldn't bear to watch the coins sold, so I did the next best thing – I took an audio tape recorder and taped the whole auction for him. When I got home, I let him listen to it. He listened for a while, but then didn't seem to have any interest in listening to the rest of it, so I just left the tapes with him.

The auction went smoothly and I was surprised by the amount of interest and spirited bidding. There were several "atta boy" at the end of many price-bidding wars. James told me later on that is what the dealers say to one another when they think the buyer in the crowd paid too much for the item for which he was bidding. To hear a chorus of "atta boy" means, "We think you got bagged."

When it was all over and the proceeds tallied, the collection "fetched," as they say, a total of $965,000. Kagin's said it was a great success and that it was the highest prices those coins sold for in history. While I have no doubt the coins would "fetch" a lot more today, it is also true that to duplicate the projects which were built by the proceeds would cost a lot more.

When I returned home and gave James a report of the trip, along with the tapes, I asked him how he felt, knowing his coins were sold. I will never forget his response: "You drink the same water, you breathe the same air." The thought was – not much changes. I could tell he felt a great deal of satisfaction in having made the gift, as though a great load was lifted off his shoulders.

James was invited for the groundbreaking at the school. I picked him up and drove him over, for the building of the school gymnasium and additional classrooms proceeded in earnest once the projects had been funded. Progress could be seen almost daily and it wasn't long before the gym and the classrooms were complete. The headmaster called and said they were going to have a dedication of the new gym and classrooms and requested that I bring James over to the ceremony and ask him to say a few words. When we got to the ceremony, there was a microphone and PA system on a small platform, and it seemed like all the schoolteachers and students were present, along with other VIPs. James had asked me about what to say on the way over, and I said the best speeches on this type of occasion are usually short and then offered some suggestions.

When called on, he responded by saying that he "never had any children of his own, but through his gift he would have an opportunity to have a part in the lives of many children for a long time to come." There he was, dressed in his summer pants, gray shirt and ugly tie, with a sport coat that almost matched the pants, making it a suit, dispensing profound words in a raspy voice that every one knew rang true. There is a plaque that hangs on the wall of the gym even today, marking that dedication event and recognizing James for his gift.

As the years rolled by I visited James every month and delivered his monthly annuity check. It was a regular event and we both looked forward to the meeting. In addition, I would pick James up once in a while and take him to lunch at a nice local restaurant. It was a big treat for him, and so I made sure that on his birthday and other special holidays and events that he got out to lunch. Whether it was for lunch or just a routine monthly visit when I would take him his check, James would always be ready, looking forward to the visit. There he would be showered; shaved, and dressed in either his summer or winter pants, gray shirt and ugly tie, with the coat at the ready position, beaming from ear to ear. His greetings would always be the exact same words, "do come in, do come in," as he greeted me at the door, which could only lead me to believe that he sat there waiting and watching for me to pull up in his driveway. Our conversations would cause the time to pass quickly and oftentimes James' sister would come and join us.

When I would take him out to lunch, people would stare at us, as I'm sure they thought I had picked up some homeless bum off the street and brought him in to eat. He would, however, be shaved, showered, and his hair would be trimmed and never too long. While not shined, his brogans would be black.

Coming back from lunch on one occasion, I decided we should stop in and see the building projects again now that they were completely decorated and in use by the children. We pulled up outside, just wandered in and began to look around. A teacher took the time to explain to a student that the old man "over there" (pointing to us) was the one who gave the money to build the gym the student had just enjoyed her class in that hour. The little student, who was about nine, then approached James and said she wanted to thank him for giving the money for her gymnasium. James looked down at her, shook her hand and said, "You're welcome." The little girl turned on her heels and ran away to the dressing room to change and get ready for her next class. While James never said anything about it later, I knew it meant a lot to him. His prophecy of having a part in the lives of children came true that day before his eyes.

In addition to my monthly visits, others from the church visited James and his sister regularly. The ladies would bake him a cake once in a while and would visit. James used to brag about the visits when I would subsequently come to see him. The deacons in the church took over the care and maintenance of the house. James' sister died after a short illness and then James was by himself. His sister left the house to the church by her will, but requested that James be given a life estate and be allowed to live there as long as he could manage by himself. Meals on Wheels and weekly shopping trips by church members kept the refrigerator stocked. In addition, a maid was hired to do some house-keeping and fix lunch.

After awhile James got sick and needed to go to the hospital. As a veteran, he went to the Veterans Hospital where he died after a short stay. James had lived about six and a half years after his gift of coins. I visited him at the hospital during his last days, but he was in a coma and I am not sure he recognized my voice. I would like to think he did and that he enjoyed our last visit together for he died shortly thereafter. I shipped his remains to Topeka where he is buried next to his parents and sisters.

Not many people remember James anymore. Not very many realize what an impact he and the few gold coins his father started out with have had in the kingdom of Christ. Let me share some with you.

- The addition of the gymnasium and the class-rooms now has over one thousand students per year using the facilities. Out of the student body, over the last twenty years, have come CEO's, doctors, lawyers, legislators and leaders in many industries, including preachers and full time missionaries, as well as teachers and military leaders. James facilitated them all.

- In addition, a portion of the gift was used to fund a fledgling television ministry called The Coral Ridge Hour, featuring Dr. D James Kennedy and the Coral Ridge Presbyterian Church. That ministry is now seen by hundreds of millions of people in 25,000 cities across America and in many foreign countries throughout the world, every week.

- Finally, a small portion of the gift was used to fund the creation of teaching materials which were produced to facilitate the teaching of pastors and key laymen so that they can train their church members how to teach others to share the Good News of Christ through a ministry called Evangelism Explosion. EE, as it is called, is now used in every nation in the world as of 1996, thirty years after his gift of coins.

One of my prized possessions is a Kagin's catalogue personally autographed to me by James. He wrote as his verse with it, John 3:16. The Scripture address was quite appropriate; you see James knew about giving. I don't hear any "atta boys" James.

## CHAPTER 6

# The Means God Provides

How many gold pieces or rare coins were in the gift that the Corinthians promised to Paul for the work of the Church and the poor in Jerusalem? I believe that whatever the gifts, they were above and beyond the regular weekly giving Paul had instructed the Church to give. Now having notified Paul and the brethren of their intent to give this gift, it became important that they follow through. As they were earnest in their love for him, Paul wanted the church to excel in the grace of giving. "*I am not commanding you* (i.e., going to talk a whole lot about it to you,) but he wanted to test just how sincere they were about this gift they said they were going to give.

If there is a standard of measurement in these matters, it is the Lord Jesus Christ himself, Paul writes: *though he was rich, yet for your sakes he became poor, so that you through his poverty might become rich*" (2 Corinthians 8:9). Consider how he had it all, gave up his riches and power and then gave of himself on the cross so that through his abject poverty we might become rich.

The more you think about it, the clearer it becomes. The principle is this: <u>Giving activates the power of God and a faith promise pledge is exactly what God gave to the world</u>. Paul wants the Corinthians to grasp the principle because it is life changing. *"Here is my advice about what is best for you in this matter"* (2 Corinthians 8:10). The word "advice" may also be translated judgment or consent. *"In this matter"* refers to the Corinthians' gift and the whole matter of giving. "This is what I think about your situation and my best judgment about what you should do in regard to it." That is how we might say it in a little different style today. Paul knows they are taking a huge step in spiritual maturity and he is now going to take the rest of the chapter eight and nine and discuss <u>the means, the men, the method, and the model for giving</u>. In short, he is going to give them all they need in the way of encouragement to complete the generous promise pledge ("having been promised blessing"), as the original language would say it. (2 Corinthians 9:5).

The means God provided each individual is the basis for the promise pledge, but what changes the means to an offering, is the willingness on the part of each individual and then the resolve of each donor, to actually make the gift. In each capital campaign there will always be a gap between what is pledged or promised and what is actually received. Once again, I have no research on which to base the observation except for what I have seen in one local church and what I learned by talking with leaders of other similar churches. Once again, the 80-20 rule comes into play with

80-90 percent of the pledged amount actually being gifted and received. And again, a large percentage of the total will be the gifts in kind which are gifted (by the donors) after pledging them. The gift is acceptable, Paul tells us *"according to what one has, not according to what he does not have"* (2 Corinthians 8:12). What you do, with what you have, is the principle element of the transaction.

You may recall the parable of the talents found in Matthew 25:14-30. It is the story of a man going on a journey, who called his servants in and gave them some money to manage. One received over $5,000; one received over $2,000 and one over $1,000, in today's currency. Notice "the man" doesn't tell them what to do with the money. It simply says *" he entrusted to them his property"* But in verse 27 of Matthew, chapter 25, he says, *"You should have put my money on deposit with the bank so that when I returned I would have received it back in interest."* Certain truths are so self- evident that it is obvious how one should conduct himself with regard to it.

Perhaps the classic example of this point is that man looks at creation, and in the light of creation he knows by the complexity of design and the vastness of the universe that there has to be a Creator. Like all self-evident truth whereby man has to confront a God that is holy and omnipotent, he rationalizes the circumstance to justify the position he has taken even though he knows it is wrong. The fact is all of us have done it. In the case of creation, man lies to himself and says what exists is a result of evolution, which now flies in the face of scientific revelation after revelation and is downright embarrassing to the pseudo scientist who finds himself the storyteller in a fairy tale for adults.

"Diogenes recapitulates Philogenes," one psuedo-intel-lectual proclaimed as he regurgitated to me a phrase he was forced to memorize at Columbia University. It was a chief tenet in his belief in evolution, and postulates that man grows a tail in the mother's womb as he is formed, but subsequently jettisons the tail before he is born, thus re-enacting the evolution of the human species itself. Little did my friend know that even the World Book Encyclopedia debunked that myth and goes on to point out how the lie got started? I started to tell my friend how wrong he was, but the timing was not good. He was a complete devotee of evolu-tion, also my boss.

How convenient for him. Just rationalize creation away, because if creation is a fact, there has to be a Creator to whom man must be accountable. Such was the case with the "wicked lazy servant," our Lord tells about in this parable. The servant rationalized his situation, lied to himself about his accountability, and then hoped everything would turn out all right. The servant even concocted a fairy tale to go along with his position. He told the master he was afraid, but the master said it was because he was wicked and lazy and it was a result of his sinful nature, that he indulged. Hasn't it been the same since the beginning when Adam said to God, *"The woman that you gave me"* (Genesis 3:12) made me do it? The woman said, *"The serpent beguiled me"* (v. 3). We as people always seem to come up with an excuse.

Paul knew that is what he was dealing with in the Corinthian Church, *"that your eager willingness to do it may be matched by your completion of it, according to your*

66

*means.*" It is the tag "according to your means" which changes things. The measurement now shifts from quantity to quality, so to speak. It's not how much did you give, but how much did you give relative to what you have? *"According to what one has, not according to what he does not have"* (2 Corinthians 8:12). The verb "has" in the text is in the present active subjunctive tense in the original language. It means what you have or don't have, **now!**

The principle is seen again in Scripture by the widow's offering in Luke 21:1-4. The widow put in two small copper coins, and the Lord said, *"I tell you the truth. This woman has put in more than all the others. All these people gave gifts out of their wealth, but she gave out of her poverty, she put in all she had to live on."* You would think that Jesus would call the disciples over and say to them, "You see that guy over there? He just gave a huge gift – a large sum of money. We would say today, "Let's name the treasury after him." In actuality, the guy had so much money that what he gave amounted to a tip rather than a tithe. How many people do you know like the widow who was commended?

I saw one of those small copper coins one time – we call it the "widow's mite." Who else but James would have it? The coin was an excellent specimen about the size of the tip of my little finger. James said there were only a few known to exist in America – perhaps the world – and most had pieces broken off of them. I don't really know what happened to the coin, but I remember thinking at the time, "I would like to have one of those sometime just to use for teaching purposes...besides collecting."

I was really impressed by the fact that the Lord of the

Universe would take the time to commend someone for giving so little, but the giving was relative to what she had and that, of course, made the difference. While he was writing to individuals, I think it is important to keep in mind Paul was writing to the entire church of God in Corinth, together with all the saints throughout Achaia. Their lessons are our lessons today.

# Church Administration of Funds

The principle of giving, then, not only applies to individuals who make up the church, but to the church itself. As we read about the principle of gathering and distributing, it is obvious if one receives an abundance he is to share with the one who gathered little, so he does not have too little (2 Corinthians 8:15). If this then applies to churches, and I believe it does, one really has to look at what his church is doing in the way of benevolence. It would break down into three different areas for today's Church in America:

- The first area is that of local outreach with the gospel, funding for personnel, materials to share Christ in the local church center of influence, i.e., the local community. It would, of course, include the pastoral staff, salaries, and management of the local church. More than that, it needs to include underwriting church programs, that go out into the local community and bring people to church where they can hear the claims of Christ. This may range from a music program of a special artist making a guest appearance to a lay-based evangelism program.

- The second type of outreach is line item missionary benevolence as a part of the church itemized budget.
- The third area would be a program to care for the poor in the local church area. It is in this third area most churches in America come up short, which is nothing new because if the churches had been doing it all along we would have a different welfare system than we have today.

Very few members get a chance to determine where funds are going to be spent. It doesn't hurt to ask questions of those who are making the decisions and to be a part of a church that is true to God's Word. It is a far different situation for those who are in charge, however, for those overseers who make the decisions where to spend the funds, that God provides through tithes and offerings of His people. In the parable of the shrewd manager found in Luke 16:1-13, the Lord sets forth the essence of the parable in verse 11 by saying, *"So if you have not been trustworthy handling worldly wealth, who will trust you with true riches?"* In verse 12, *"And if you have not been trustworthy with someone else's property, who will give you property of your own."* This parable was directed specifically to the church leaders, because we read in verse 14, *"The Pharisees who loved money were sneering at Jesus."*

As an Elder in charge of stewardship, I read this text not only with trepidation but also with a renewed commitment to remain diligent and trustworthy, balancing the church general budget with a judicious mind set. Yet, at the same time, funding and advancing programs which evangelize at the local and foreign venues, while simultaneously caring for the poor. It is not an easy task. There are some major pitfalls, that need to be avoided.

The first is what I call the "It's just like a business mentality." It goes something like this; you hire a manager to be the church administrator and give him full reign to handle the affairs of the church in a "businesslike" manner. It usually is someone who comes out of the business world and into the church with a big reputation and often an ego to match. Unless you have a very special godly man, what you do in a case like this is light a stick of dynamite and throw it in the front door of the church. This is especially true if the administrator has not been a Christian for a long time.

Usually the first thing the new administrator does is find what he perceives to be the deadwood that is not carrying their load. The next thing he does is bring in his own people. He wants the new people to be really good at what they do because it will reflect on him, for he is the one who put them on his "team." To get the kind of people he wants, he has to come to the conclusion he has to pay up to get good competent people. If he thinks he might have a hard time selling the church leaders they need to pay more to "get" these people, he will usually make an arbitrary and unilateral move claiming that this is what he was hired to do – bring management skills to bear and "run the church like a business."

The easiest way to look good right away then is to reallocate line item expenses on the income and expense statement so a year to year actual comparison will reveal that expenses in certain categories are lower in the current year than they were in the prior year. Q.E.D., The new administrator is really doing a good job – look at how much lower the expenses are in this category compared with the prior year. Illusionists call it slight of hand; professionals call it creative accounting. Mysteriously, however the overall expenses of the church go up, but that, of course, is due to inflation, utilities, replacement of equipment which was worn out, extraordinary one-time expense, Hale-Bopp…you name it.

In the meantime, the stick of dynamite in the front door explodes and the people who were fired leave the church, along with all their friends and relatives who are "shocked" at the way the terminated employees were treated. Moreover, they tell all their friends, who tell all their friends, etc., and the multiplier kicks in at the fourth level, as usual. In the meantime, the other staff, now fearing for their jobs, get stressed out from avoiding the hatchet man. They quickly update their resumes or prepare new ones, put them in the mail, make some discreet calls, and the beat goes on.

After having seized power, the next step for the new administrator is to consolidate his power. This is usually done through the writing of job descriptions, personnel manuals, and preparing a new staff line reporting chart that shows the new administrator at the top and everyone underneath reporting to him, or a middle manager who reports to him. Position reassignments and the creation of new positions, that consolidate and retitle others, are some of the techniques employed. This strategy often requires the attitude of a middle linebacker because some of these changes don't come easy. Process re-engineering is the buzzword, but the end result is bitter feelings, divisions and chaos. While the title of administrator is used here, the same circumstances and conditions may exist under an assistant pastor or a music director. The title isn't important; like the verse says, *"by their fruits you know them."*

# CHAPTER 8

# The Art of Delegating

There are three elements of delegation, which the overseer must employ in the oversight of the church funds. These elements may be seen in several places in Scripture. Let's look at the components of good delegation and then see some examples of them in action in Scripture. The first element is that of responsibility. When a job is assigned, a complete picture of what the job entails should be given so that there is no doubt in the mind of the employee just what it is he/she is responsible for in the performance of the job. It is usually done with a written job description that is given to the employee. Another name for it is a "position charter."

The second element of delegation is that of authority. Often an employee will be given a job to do but not the authority to accomplish the task. Let me give a very simplistic illustration, that can be adapted to any situation. Supervisor gives an employee a task: "Go change the light bulb in the men's room." Seems simple enough! Employee goes to the men's restroom to change the bulb and removes the burned out, 150-watt bulb. He goes to the supply room for a replacement, but finds there are only 50-watt bulbs in inventory. He goes back to his supervisor to see what he should do – put a 50-watt bulb in or go to the store and buy some 150-watt bulbs. He had heard cash was a little tight at the church.

In the meantime, the supervisor had to go to an all-day meeting. He left instructions with his secretary that he is only to be disturbed in the event of an emergency. The employee is so informed. With other work to do, the employee embarks on his daily routine with the thought that he will wait until tomorrow to see what the boss wants to do about bulbs.

The next day the supervisor returns to his office and, as usual, he arrives about 8 a.m., an hour early. At 8:30, having finished his third cup of coffee, he grabs his newspaper and heads for the men's' room, only to discover there is no light. He remembers telling the employee he wanted the light changed, and now he is furious that it didn't get done.

The question is: Whose fault is it? Not the employee's, but the supervisor's. Why? When the Supervisor gave the employee the <u>responsibility</u>, he should also have given him the <u>authority</u> necessary to go along with it. He should have told him to change the light bulb in the men's room and if the right size bulb was not available, to get some petty cash from finance, go to the store and buy some. Most people would leave it at that, having combined elements one and two of the delegation process – responsibility and authority.

The third element of the delegation process, however,

separates the players from the wannabes, the really good manager from the mediocre ones. It is the element of <u>accountability</u>. While most people know the word in the context of management, few understand how to implement it. Accountability is not something, that occurs after the fact or a line responsibility of who is accountable to whom and for what; it is an early element of the delegation process. Reporting and accountability are often thought to be one and the same but far from it. Reporting is a procedure where accountability takes place.

Let's consider once again the case of the supervisor, the employee, and the light bulb. The proper way to delegate that task would be to say, "Change the light bulb in the men's room. If we don't have any bulbs the right size, get some petty cash from finance, go to the store, and buy some. After you have finished the job, leave a note on my desk or tell my secretary what you did". The employee understands the responsibility, has the authority, and now has the accountability to report on the task assigned.

Consider how the nobleman who was to be made king handled the delegation in Luke 19:27. In this parable the man of noble birth is going to go away *"to a distant country to be appointed king and then to return."* We read that he called ten of his servants and gave them minas (responsibility). *"Put this money to work," he said* (authority). He said to invest the money, *"until I come back"*. When he returned, *"He sent for the servants to whom he had given the money in order to find out what they had gained with it."* He held them accountable.

While the example of the light bulb is simplistic, as I

said, let's take it now to the next level. Who were the servants to whom the nobleman gave the money? I submit they were the overseers of his church. While it is dangerous to take a section of a parable and consider it apart from the one central thought of the parable, the context of delegation is accurate. "What have you done with what I gave you?"

As I considered that text of the ten servants, I have often wondered what the first servant did to earn "ten more" than the servant who finished second with "five more." The first servant received praise, a reward and a title. The second only receive a reward. Whatever he did, the first servant was clearly the best manager and, accordingly, received the biggest reward. In each of the examples we have looked at, God provided the means for ministry, but only the first servant was called trustworthy.

It is uncalled for to speculate why the second did not receive a title "good servant" or a commendation "trustworthy." But from what I can see, there are a lot more type two churches out there than type ones. One thing is for certain; the king didn't call the banker in to testify on what he did to earn the interest he paid to the servant. When the overseer is called to account, he can't say, "My banker didn't do a good job and that is why I don't have a big return to present to you." Stated another way: "I am not willing to take the ministry God has given to me and hand it over to someone so they can operate it "like a business." The reason is simple – it's not a business; it's a ministry.

# CHAPTER 9

# Compensation in the Church Today

This brings me to the second point of managing the means God has provided – church salaries. Salaries are a touchy, delicate topic in the church today because it is easy to err on either side of what is right. I knew a church where the elders of the church visited staff ministers once a year in their homes. The object was to meet the needs and concerns of the pastors in order to encourage them and support them physically, as well as spiritually. When one such team was visiting the minister's house they asked, "Is there anything you need that we can get for you?"

"We are just fine," the godly man replied. "We lack for nothing." As the team completed their visit, they turned to leave and one of the team members asked the minister, "What can we get you for your birthday coming up?" The minister replied, "I would like to have another pair of shoes.

This pair I have is falling apart." The pastor only had one pair of shoes. When they looked at his compensation package, it was pretty obvious why he had only one pair of shoes; they were not paying him enough money. They felt sick. Needless to say this guy was not going to complain. He was a Godly man, and whatever the Lord supplied for him in the way of means was just fine with him. He would make do. God on the other hand might not be too pleased that his man was not adequately compensated when there was certainly enough money in the church. That scenario is one end of the scale.

At the other end is where the staff is paid too much – particularly the non-ordained positions. Any rationale, which says church staff should be paid the same as comparable positions in the secular business world is not a valid thesis. There are three reasons:

- First it's not a secular business; it is a ministry, and as such, it requires a close walk with Christ because your every move is going to be scrutinized carefully. As such, you are expected to model the Lord as he modeled the lifestyle of holiness. *"Be on your guard against all kinds of greed; a man's life does not consist in the abundance of his possessions"* (Luke 12:15). One sure sign that you are in ministry because you want to be in ministry is that you are willing to work for less than you could earn in a comparable job in the secular business world. It is a simple test – you are there because you want to be there, not because you need the job.

- The second reason I believe you should earn less money is because it doesn't become a stumbling block to others, both inside and outside the church. If those inside the church, staff and regular members, know that the person is being paid too much relative to the secular world, they become resentful and offended – resentful that their money is going to pay that big salary and offended that those in charge are paying that much.
- A third reason for paying less is that the money goes further and additional ministry is available. If all of the money generated by scaled back salaries are pooled together in a fund created by saving 10% from each position, (if there are ten staff positions with a mean income of $40,000) with the savings of 10% there is an additional position available paying $40,000 which otherwise would not be available.

One might muse and say that the difference between servant number one who gained 100 percent, and servant number two who earned 50 percent, was that servant number two didn't control his expenses. Marginal expenses will always rise to meet marginal revenues. It's an immutable law in the business universe. If pay raises are given as a percent across the board, the raises will always benefit those who are making the most.

There will always be the temptation in ministry to say this person had a job in the secular world that paid "X". Therefore, because of his qualifications, education, and experience, we need to pay that much to hire the person. It may very well be that the person being considered is worth "X," but our position is only worth "Y." Therefore, because we are not willing to pay more than the position is worth, that person should go somewhere else, where he or she can be paid what he or she wants. It certainly isn't in the ministry.

Each church knows what the cost of living is in its particular market and it generally is a factor of real estate values versus other sections of the country for comparable housing. Often someone moving to South Florida on the East Coast is surprised how much higher housing can be while the other costs of living, such as clothes, are about the same as the rest of the country, but on balance with higher overall prices. God provides the means and then calls us to account as to how we use the means.

CHAPTER 10

# The Men God Chooses –
# Development Directors
# and Others

In 2 Corinthians 8:16 Paul begins a discussion of the men he has chosen for the task of completing the collection of the promise pledge by considering Titus and his attitude in the whole matter. The response is to praise God because it is he who put into the heart of Titus the same concern for the Corinthians that Paul had for them.

In church after church I have seen the pastoral staff surrounded by some good men – sometimes, as the marines say, "a few." But it seems the larger the church, the larger the core of good men God has raised up to assist the pastoral staff. Often the pastors have a hard time determining who are those responsible men God has sent and who are the ones to avoid. For instance, in comes a guy who really looks good on the surface – maybe he has just relocated to the area or comes as a staff referral. There is a tendency on the part of the pastors to think, "This is a man God has sent to assist in ministry." Then it turns out the guy is one big bag of trouble.

How, then, does a pastor know whether an individual is a real asset or a disaster? How does a Session know if a brother who is recommended to be a Deacon or Elder is the right man? This question of personnel selection is the difference between a good administrative Pastor and one who is a poor judge of character. The Pastor who is a poor judge ends up having to fire the staff member after much chagrin that could have been avoided. The Session or the Diaconate has to live with their mistake for the life of the officer's term before they can get rid of a dud. (In Presbyterian circles it is often a term of four years.) The answer to these questions is: through careful background screening and due diligence in personal interviews with references and people at the prospects prior employment.

When a new employee comes on board, there should also be an understanding between the employer and the new hire that a probationary period of ninety days will be in effect while each evaluates the other. The new employee determines if he likes the position and the employer evaluates the performance of the new employee. Applicable State Law will determine each situation. The Apostle Paul evaluated his team and knew them well.

It's important to understand Titus's role in the ministry of the Corinthians. He is Paul's right hand man for the Corinthian Church. He is to direct the business affairs for the promised gift and he is going to get some help to do it.

Most successful churches have a business director who oversees a lot of the day-to-day operations of the church and removes a big burden from the pastoral staff. The pastors can go about their daily duties of ministering to the flock, without having to worry about the heat/air conditioning, for example.

There is another key player in the larger churches and ministries – a type of Titus. The title of this person is the Director of Development. A necessity for advanced giving, called developmental giving, that I will discuss later, the director of development is a businessman who is skilled in developing large gifts through tax planning with wealthy donors. He may represent the church when a donor wishes to make a gift in kind to the church – for example, a house or condo or other tangible asset. The church or ministry has three options to secure developmental personnel.

The first is to go out and hire an established skilled representative who is working or has worked at another place and has developed the knowledge necessary to plan, make contacts, and be successful. The problem of doing it this way is twofold.

They usually want too much money to make the move because they know what they are worth to an organization, and there are numerous demands for their services. The second is that they often bring with them a lot of baggage, which is not known when they are hired. I know of two such men, and there is a lot to be learned from looking at their history. The first was a former director of development at a Christian university. He was middle-aged, married, good looking, handled himself well, and dressed impeccably. He was a guy who just reeked of success, and no doubt, in just listening to him, if we were to hire him, which we did practically on the spot, we would be successful. He told us of the many millions he had raised for the Christian university and the large salary he required could easily be covered once he had a chance to unfurl his skills. We were fortunate to get him, we were told. Without so much as a referral call or background check he was on board and working in his office. It didn't take long for us to figure out our much heralded acquisition was a dud. The staff found him to be irritable, hard to get along with, and very demanding. Moreover, his expertise turned out to be far less than anticipated. After a brief stay he moved on the greener pastures where his "expertise" could be put to greater use. I never heard from him again but neither did I try to follow his career.

Another development director was hired by a church when the man stated he needed to relocate because of some health problems his wife was having. He was knowledgeable, was not asking for a huge salary, and had a really nice, likeable personality. In fact, he set himself up with a couple of other local ministries whereby they could pick up some of the salary and benefit expenses. This man had worked for the Salvation Army, but once again the church that hired him did not do enough of a background check or make reference calls.

Such behavior must be typical in church and Christian ministries because we tend to believe people when they tell us something and we don't really do an exhaustive search, as we should. We think "we need to grab this guy because if we don't, he has some other offers he is considering and we are going to lose him." I think a search committee should run the other way every time they hear something like that tale. It's one of the disaster tip-offs I am about to discuss when hiring stewardship staff or development directors.

As for the Salvation Army man — soon after coming on board the church and other related organizations, he announced he had been ordained and preferred to be addressed by his title of Reverend. He had sent a few hundred dollars to a mail order "church," and the "church" sent him a certificate proclaiming him to be an "ordained minister." No requirement for ordination other than cash. Of course the tax benefits of being an "ordained minister" were available. I am sure if a money order had been sent along with an application signed by my dog with her paw print, they would have "ordained" my female West Highland Scottish Terrier "The Right Reverend Tootsie Muffin."

The church that hired the director, an old-line denomination conservative church, should have canned the guy on the spot, having already shown himself to be a fraud and deceitful. The church seemed to forget that lying and stealing go hand in hand. Instead, the church took "dumb" to the next level, and at the insistence of the director, listed him in the church bulletin as "Reverend" on the church staff. It looked good in the bulletin having another "Pastor" on staff. You can imagine the impact the director had calling on donors out of town, and even in town, as the "Reverend" from the Church.

Left uncontrolled and essentially unaccountable, a Director of Development can wreak havoc, that can take a long time to undo if he strays from the straight and narrow. Changing beneficiaries to include not only his employer, but also some for his "ministry," i.e. himself is only one of the things I was told the Director did wrong.

If a church has a Director of Development, a committee of businessmen, such as a Certified Financial Planner (CFP), stockbrokers, attorneys, CPAs, or insurance agents should oversee his work. The committee should monitor the activities of the Director to see that the activities are diligent and honorable. Copies of all documents should be filed at the church central office where only the Pastor or his secretary has a key. This means keeping the Director out of the deferred document files unless there is someone else present when the files are made available to the Director of Development; which they need to be on regular basis so he can review and prospect.

By doing it that way the church staff has control of the documents for review by the professionals who can look for abuses in the documents that may be drafted or modified into them. The review should include all known developmental gifts, particularly the deferred giving file at least annually. A recommended list of attorneys who are preferred by the church for the drafting of documents should be used, except when donors have an attorney they insist on using.

Drafting attorneys should send the original documents to the church and the original documents should be kept in either a fireproof box in a safe at the church or in a box at the local bank. While some attorneys suggest that the documents be kept in the donor's fireproof box or at the bank, many attorneys suggest the donor utilize the attorney's vault. "I will keep the original in my safe deposit box at the bank and I am going to give you as many copies as you need," the drafting attorney often proclaims. "There will be no charge to you for providing this safekeeping."

The reason for this benevolent gesture is not readily apparent to the donor but the attorney wants to keep the original document because the attorney who files the will with the Clerk of Courts is the attorney of record for administration of the estate. As such, the attorney is entitled to charge probate fees. One study showed that on average, the percentage of the gross federal estate as a national average, the probate fee, called administrative expenses, was 8%.

One attorney in south Florida had the original trust document of a charitable remainder unitrust, which left a large amount of money to a local university law school. The attorney refused to distribute the funds in the trust until he was paid a fee of approximately one million dollars. He got his fee but I understand the attorney was subsequently disbarred, although I have no proof of that fact. The story certainly was front-page headlines in the local newspaper for a while.

While there are many good directors of development, these are but two of the many stories told by organizations that went out and hired directors. Still many organizations have had a good experience by going into the marketplace and hiring one. The most successful long- term approach to having a director of development is to "grow your own." That appears to be the route Paul took with Titus. The primary reason was that Titus had a heart for ministry. (2 Corinthians 8:17). It showed in his enthusiasm and his initiative.

Perhaps the best of the homegrown variety was a man

who was stockbroker at a major New York Stock Exchange firm. Jerry and his wife, who had been a dancer and was headed for a professional dancing career in New York and Hollywood screen test before getting married, came to Christ as a result of the outreach ministry of a local church.

After a couple of years of growth in Christ, Jerry found he could no longer work in his position as a stockbroker with a clear conscience, so he quit his job and started a painting company, primarily painting the cement tile roofs of homes in South Florida. The roofs in Florida are mostly white cement tiles to reflect the heat and are heavy enough to keep from being blown off the roof in some of the high winds prevalent to the area. A hard working roof painter can make a good living in South Florida, but it is a job that's hard on the body.

When a position opened in the business office of the church, he applied for it and was hired because, like Titus, he had much enthusiasm. A decision was made by the Stewardship Committee that since Jerry had such a good background in business and was doing some development work on his own initiative, he would be given the additional title of Director of Development. So he had the authority to go along with the responsibility. As a representative of the church, he attended a school for directors of development sponsored by an organization, which promoted and trained personnel for a specialized area of ministry. In addition he enrolled at the College of Financial Planning in Denver, Colorado, and took classes of the curriculum at a local university where the courses were taught. He finished his

CFP designation and was doing quite well in the department at the church.

He was really happy and in the course of his work called on a local businessman who had decided to create a charitable remainder unitrust and fund it with a large ranch that the prospective donor owned in west Texas. Several organizations were in the running for this prize, but the donor's secretary was a member of the church. As Director of Development, Jerry called the donor and convinced him to gift the ranch to the director's church. The donor considered and then agreed to do it. The farm sold for $500,000 and it was a much-needed gift at the time.

Shortly after that, the Director of Development started acting a little strange and was not himself at all. A brain scan at a local hospital confirmed what was suspected – the Director had a large tumor growing in his head. A decision was made to operate right away and remove it. There was a 50/50 chance it would turn out benign.

I waited outside the operating room with his wife and her mother. When the doctor came out, he sat down with Jerry's wife and told her the bad news straight out – the tumor was malignant. It was of a type that grows very fast and they were not able to get it all without turning him into a vegetable because the tumor was systemic and into the brain. The doctor gave him about six months to live and told the family he would die in a coma without feeling any pain. Jerry actually lived a year but the doctor had the rest of it right. He left a wife, grown son and two beautiful daughters, aged 10 and 12. I helped his wife clean out his office and put his stuff in boxes. We just looked at each other. This just didn't make any sense to us. He had just started to do so well as the Director of Development. I can only presume that God had an opening for a Director of Development in heaven and he wanted this one to start right away.

In addition to going out and hiring a Director of Development or growing your own, like we have just looked at, a third way is to hire an independent organization to come in and represent your church or organization locally. There are many fine companies who do this kind of work on a fee basis. They will come to your organization and put on a seminar for deferred giving, or they will do a mailing to your organization's list of donors and call on those who respond. Sometimes they will just work on a referral basis where someone inquires of your organization about making a gift, or leaving a legacy through a will. If you refer the call to the outside third party organization, they will call on the prospect, send you a call report of what transpired at the meeting, and the results, if any. While this method has the advantage of a low cost one-time call fee, which varies in price, it has the disadvantages of not really being a part of the organization they represent. I have been a part of an organization, which has used this method of development, and it leaves a lot to be desired.

I know a man who was filling in for an Executive Director who had been terminated from a large television ministry. While there was a search committee looking for a replacement, the substitute was in his office one day when the outside development organization's new representative came to call on his account to make sure his organization, which was serving as the outside director of development, was not in jeopardy of losing its contract. The representative could have, with a little makeup, passed as a clown the way he was dressed and with his appearance. After chatting briefly with the representative, the substitute executive made a mental note that the representative was a poor ambassador and a change needed to be made. Of the three ways to obtain a director of development, each organization must determine which is best for it. If at all possible, I recommend an organization grow their own. From many standpoints it is more rewarding in the long run.

# CHAPTER 11

# Unnamed Brothers: Trustworthy Businessmen

Along with Titus, Paul sent two men who are unnamed, and the subject of much speculation, to complete the promise pledge gift for the church. It was necessary that Titus have some help. Once again, as an Elder in charge of stewardship at a mega church, I understand their role, which I believe was to liquidate the gifts in kind which were promised as an integral part of the overall amount pledged. The first of Titus's two companions is *"the brother who is praised by all the churches for his service to the gospel."* We see that helper number one had been *"chosen by the churches to accompany us as we carry the offering which we administer in order to honor the Lord Himself and to show our eagerness to help."* (2 Corinthians 8: 18-19) The reader is left to speculate on just whom these men may be and why did the apostle not name them outright.

Another question is why did the churches in one region choose him? All of those offering an opinion as to who these anonymous men may be, seem to have only one thing in common, nobody knows who they are. The most popular guess seems to be Luke. That guess has as much of a case against it however, and only conjecture is left as an answer. I would like to offer my conjecture then and say that it was neither Luke nor the other popular choices Barnabas or Silas, but that both unnamed brothers were businessmen—men with expertise in trading and markets, money and banking. I have come to this conclusion by asking myself who would my church send on a mission such as this today? The answer would be perhaps an assistant pastor who was well known and a couple of businessmen to help him. Why businessmen? Because their expertise would be needed to liquidate the gifts in kind, negotiate the sales and close the deals.

You remember in Acts 5:1-11, the story of Annanias and Sapphira, who sold a piece of property, kept back part of the money for themselves and came and laid the balance of it at the apostles' feet? The narrative concludes in verse 11: ... *"great fear seized the whole church and all who heard about these events.* What Annanias and Sapphira gave to the church was a piece of land, which they had sold and then lied about the amount of money they received, so the word spread quickly. That is to say, it was a gift in kind, which needed to be liquidated. Now people knew that it was because they lied to the Holy Spirit they died, but they also knew it was something to be taken very seriously when property was being gifted and sold.

Consider the fact if Paul had named the two, people may

have said; who? But by introducing them by reputation and position, i.e., *"chosen by the churches"* and *"he who proved to us that he is zealous."* Paul takes them to a higher level in the minds of the Corinthians. It is as though they went from third team back to first team specialists. Known to a lot of people or known to a lot of people by what you do: Suppose those were your choices, which would you choose? These men were chosen not only because of their expertise but because they were above reproach, having already been tested with the handling of money and found faithful, they could now be commended to others, the principle we have already looked at in the parables.

The reason Paul delegates the task to these three men is found clearly in verse 20 and 21 *"We want to avoid any criticism of the way we administer the liberal gift." "For we are taking pains to do what is right not only in the eyes of the Lord but also in the eyes of men."* The handling of the gift would be an occasion of criticism and Paul was too smart to get into that trap. Perhaps John Calvin said it best: "There is nothing which is more apt to lay one open to sinister imputations than the handling of public money." Of course this includes public officials and government workers as well as the church but there is nothing more repugnant than the thought that people who are doing without and making sacrifices to give have their money wasted by the overseers of the gift.

When the famed Tel-Evangelist Jim Bakker scandal broke, the mismanagement of the funds in the ministry was the part Christians had a hard time dealing with as the facts were released. I found the part about having the doghouse air-conditioned particularly troublesome. The nation had a field day with it because even they knew the story of the widow's mite and suggested its applications to the doghouse of course. If the Jim Bakker story was an isolated event it would be one thing, but stories of abuse seem to come up all the time, such as recently a pastor at a Baptist church in Pompano Beach, Florida was found to own a Rolls, two Mercedes, and a house in joint name with another woman who was not his wife. Needless to say it was a headline in the local newspaper. When something like that happens it hurts the cause of Christ not only locally but all over the world as well. I know for a fact that all television ministries experienced a drop in donor income as people became disappointed with television preachers in general.

I don't know about a lot of television preachers and whether they take a salary from the ministry or not but I do know of one that takes no money at all from his TV ministry. That person is Dr. D. James Kennedy, pastor of the Coral Ridge Presbyterian Church in Fort Lauderdale, Florida, host of the TV program **The Coral Ridge Hour** and also radio programs **Truths That Transform** and **The Kennedy Commentary**, a one minute radio bullet. As a founding director said: " It was a decision of the Board of Directors to leave it up to Dr. Kennedy to decide if he should be paid a salary or not. He made the decision not to ever take any salary or any other remuneration from the media programs. He also decided to turn over any royalty checks he received from books he has written which are sold on TV or radio." He also gives back all of his salary that the church pays him. His source of income is honorariums, which are paid speaking engagements, and book royalties. Dr. Kennedy makes the members laugh when he says, "How many churches have a pastor that pays the church to let him preach?" I can further attest that he drives a modest car, which the church purchased for him, and lives in a modest house that the church finally gave to him after thirty years of service. What a contrast to an air-conditioned doghouse or multiple luxury cars. No wonder God has so blessed the man!

Paul was aware of the potential for slanderous malicious gossip when he writes, *"For we are taking pains to do what is right"* (II Corinthians 8:21). The word used for "taking pains" in the original language is the word pronoeo which is made up of two words "pro" which means before and "noeo" that means to think, comprehend. With an accusative of the thing, it means to provide care beforehand. Taking pains is a great way of expressing what is going on here and the NIV translators are to be commended for this expression of pronoeo. It sometimes is a pain to do the right thing which in a case like this calls for going out of ones' way, thinking about the actions beforehand and coming up with a strategy which will avoid criticism down the road.

It goes to the heart of the matter, which is avoiding even the appearance of evil for the sake of the others conscience. And so it is that Paul commends Titus and the brothers to the Church of Corinth and lest the Corinthians think that the brothers are his representatives he reminds them that they are the *"representatives of the churches and an honor to Christ."* (2Corinthians 8:23) He reminds the Corinthians that they are the ones at bat and he asks them to display *"the reason our pride is in you"* *"so the churches can see it."*

(2Corinthians 8:24) Continuing the theme: Look! This is your show, and I have confidence in you. This statement of the purpose is twofold: to show your love for Christ by showing your love for these men and by being a role model for the other churches.

I know a Church, that has numerous occasions during the year where members have an opportunity to open their homes to various groups that are attending functions at the Church. The visitors are blessed by the love shown to them by the hosts and comment about how welcome they feel and how God's Spirit is at work in the Church. The hosts are also blessed as their vision for the work of God is expanded as they hear about what God is doing in other parts of the world. Demonstrating the "proof of their love," the hosts become spiritual partakers of the ministry of their guests. They become "givers" as found in the account of the sheep and the goats in Matthew 25 where the Lord says, *"I was a stranger and you invited me in"*. *"I was hungry and you gave me something to eat"* (Matt.25: 35). I think the subject of Christian hospitality is a subject that would make a fascinating study, i.e., how would you like to give the Creator of the universe a drink of water, and a bite to eat? Yet Christ declares, as he assumes the role of Judge of all the earth at the final judgement, *"whatever you did for one of the least of these brothers of mine, you did for me."* That's heady stuff! More about this subject later.

# CHAPTER 12

# A Classic Building Fund Campaign

Paul opens chapter 9 of 2 Corinthians by saying *"There is no need for me to write to you about this service."* The word in the Greek translated "service" is the familiar word diakonia, the root word from which we get diakonos, that means minister, or servant. Of course it is also the root word for Deacon, which is the office of sympathy and service. As used here, it is a type of compassionate love toward the needy within the Christian community and a desire to help them, which the apostle acknowledges in verse 2 of chapter 9. Paul says that he has been boasting to the Macedonians about the willingness of the Corinthian Church to give since last year, and that boast prompted the Macedonians to give, which we read about in 2 Corinthians 8:1-3. Now we start to see a principle, which may be used in fundraising in the local church. After Paul encourages the Macedonian church by telling them about the promise pledge of the Corinthians, he tells the Corinthians about the giving of the Macedonian Church. Everybody is encouraged.

I know of a modern day example, which illustrates this principle, and I would like to share it with you. A local church started to grow rapidly as the pastor faithfully proclaimed God's Word and trained his laymen how to be effective witnesses and to train others to do the same. A new sanctuary was built on a tract of land, which was purchased by the congregation. It was the first part of a two-fold expansion in which the second phase would include building a large fellowship hall with a kitchen, a big nursery, music area, pastoral offices and the like. The beautiful sanctuary was built complete with all the amenities of a first class facility. The church membership continued to mushroom until there were overflow crowds at both Sunday morning services. But like a business which expands too rapidly, and buries itself with the inability to support the expansion, the church was unable to facilitate the much needed care areas such as the demand for a large nursery, youth facilities, church dinners and the like. In addition, with a heart for ministry, the church continued to reach out with its funds.

As time passed, it became apparent that it was time to do phase two and develop the congregational facilities in order to continue to strengthen the local church. How to go about raising the funds for the expansion was a topic of much discussion. It was finally determined to hire an outside consultant to assist with the project because it was going to involve a multi-million, multi-year commitment on the part of the congregation. The Stewardship Committee recommended the hiring of Resource Services Incorporated, known as RSI, out of Dallas, Texas. The reason Resource Services Inc. was selected was because of the excellent reputation it enjoyed among the churches. Sounds a little like the two unnamed brothers, doesn't it?

RSI, as they were called, had been involved with capital campaigns in local churches for some time and the churches which were given as references, gave good reports on their experience with RSI. After some negotiation as to fees for services, a contract was signed and a team of RSI personnel went to the church with detailed plans on how to conduct a campaign. The first thing they did was share what God was doing in other churches throughout America. It was so encouraging to the local congregation to know that this is the kind of project in which God is involved. A special campaign to provide additional facilities for a local church is something God delighted in at other churches and he would do the same for their local church.

It was exactly the kind of thing that Paul did when he told the Macedonians what the Corinthians were doing and when he told the Corinthians what the Church in Macedonia had done. There is no attempt to play one church against another, as that sort of thing would be far below the nature of the apostle to try to manipulate the giving of the churches. No, it had the same effect and purpose that RSI's report to the local congregation, which included what God was doing in Baptist, Presbyterian, Methodist, and Independent churches across the land. It gave a method to achieving a goal. So now not only do we have the <u>means</u>

God provided, the <u>men</u> he uses, but the <u>method</u> used to develop it.

The method starts with a vision for the church and what God would have them to do in the area of giving. RSI uses this principle by allowing each church to develop a theme for the campaign they desire launch. In the case of the church I am talking about in this illustration, the capital campaign was titled "Finish the Dream." It was a great theme, because everyone knew that the limited facilities which they were using, were only a down payment on the facility they hoped to have as a congregation. To go ahead now and raise the funds to "finish" what they had begun so many years before was completing what they had only "dreamed" of for many years.

While the exact methodology of RSI remains confidential and proprietary, the results are certainly to be shared to the glory of God. The congregation was stirred to action, as Paul puts it in 2 Corinthians 9: 2. The word, stirred, in the original language "erethizo" means to stir up, provoke, and arouse. It can also mean embitter or irritate, which I think is fascinating because that's exactly what happened to a number of people in the congregation. They became irritated that someone was asking them to give above and beyond their normal giving in a faith promise pledge. Some were embittered enough to leave the church, so they went somewhere else. (Now after they are there don't you know that their new church is starting a fund to build a new building.)? But that is the way it has always been throughout history of the church. Some are stirred enough to give sacrificially while others get offended and leave. If you are contemplating a capital campaign in your church, remember that some will get erethizo and then some others will get erethizo, its God's way of doing it.

Whereas most capital campaigns involve a pledge over a period of time, usually three years, there will be some natural short fall in the amount pledged and the amount collected. While it will vary from church to church, once again the 80-20 to 95-5 rule will apply with 5% - 20% of the funds pledged failing to materialize. The reasons vary but include people relocating, dying, and getting unhappy, to name but a few. The reason I point this out is any campaign to expand facilities should have as an expenditure, 5% to 20% of the funds pledged as a safety net when calculating the cost. For example, a one million-dollar expenditure should have pledges of $1,200,000. Or a pledge amount of one million can carry an expenditure of $800,000.

A second reason for the cushion is that building costs tend to rise once the construction process has begun. A little change here, a little change there, you know how it goes, i.e., we really could use some magic carpet to go along with this Hale-Bopp, and pretty soon you are over budget. A classic business axiom is that marginal expenses will always rise to meet marginal revenues and that seems particularly true when it comes to building programs. If you look to spend the amount of your pledge income on your program, whatever it may be, you will have to come back at a later date and have another campaign to raise the funds that you thought you were going to get the first time, before you learned about erethizo. That is what happened to the church in the example I am discussing. While they stayed close to budget on the expense side, the pledge income fell short of projected revenue and it was tight for them for a while while they experienced the learning curve of this principle.

Another phenomenon of a capital campaign is that it takes money away from the general fund of the church. While great care is exercised in the explanation of the principle that sacrificial giving is expected to be above and beyond the regular giving, it inevitably doesn't work that way 100%. While it is true that overall giving will rise as those who have sacrificially pledged complete their pledges, there are those who will complete their pledge by taking money away from their general fund giving. No matter how much you preach that your pledge is to be above and beyond regular giving, for many it won't be – so don't be surprised that general fund revenues drop when the capital campaign starts. On the bright side, however, after the capital campaign is over, the general fund will rise to a higher amount than prior to the campaign. I believe people get blessed by God and end up giving more in the future.

As for Paul sending the brothers on ahead so that the pledge fund would be complete and *"ready as I said you would be"* (2 Corinthians 9:3). The only way that gift was going to be ready was if those businessmen and Titus liquidated those gifts in kind beforehand. He knew if they didn't go on ahead and liquidate, they would have egg on their face, *"ashamed of being so confident."* (2 Corinthians 9:4) Paul really was concerned for the church and its reputation and so he includes himself "we - not to say anything about you in the embarrassed pool. He had told the Macedonians about the generosity of the Corinthians and now his credibility was on the line as well as theirs. It was necessary that the brothers finish the "arrangements."

To those commentators who opined that these brothers going to Corinth were going to collect, they are left to answer this question; collect how? Threaten the people to give the gift? Hi, my name is Bruno the Bruiser and I'm here to collect the marker (promise). Pay up now! Absurd! The arrangements were for a "generous gift" which had been "promised" not as one grudgingly given. Here is where it gets interesting.

# CHAPTER 13

# The Original Promise Pledge

The word in the Greek text, which is translated "promised" is the word pro-epangellomai, which has as its root word Angel. A literal rendering of the text could be "*I thought to beseech the brothers in order that they go forward to you and arrange beforehand the having been promised blessing of you, this ready to be thus as a blessing and not as greediness.* Of course, the King James Version translates it "*make up beforehand your bounty whereof ye had notice before, that the same might be ready as a matter of bounty* (2 Corinthians 9:5). A lot has changed in the use of language today. When I read the NIV translation "promised" I looked up the Greek word for "promised" and then went to Dr. George Knight, a Professor at Knox Theological Seminary in Fort Lauderdale, Florida. I wanted to confirm my thesis regarding this passage. He informed me I was correct and he too found the thesis fascinating and encouraged me to develop the thought. He also said it was the same root word that appeared in Romans 1:2 where it says, *"The gospel he promised beforehand"* Epangello – bring word to, announce, promise.

The reason God loves a faith promise is because he gave us his promise through his prophets in the Holy Scriptures that we receive by faith. These are the only two places in the New Testament where that word is used in this form. When you get the thought and connect the two, you want to jump up and down; it's so clear, so practical. It combines the idea that your faith, believing what you can't see, is connected to something which will appear.

To understand just how great the promise is, we have to go back to the Garden of Eden in Genesis chapter 2 and read the account of God's instruction to Adam: *"You must not eat from the tree of the knowledge of good and evil, for when you eat of it you will surely die."* (Genesis 2:17) After Adam and Eve disobey, they are called to account by God in chapter 3:8-19. When God addresses the serpent, he tells the serpent *"I will put enmity between you and the woman and between your offspring and hers.* (Genesis 3:15) Theologians call this the pro-evangelium, the first announcement that One would come and redeem man, that God would not abandon man in his sinful state but promised to provide a Savior. God said to the serpent: *"He will crush your head and you will strike his heel"* (Genesis 3:15b). So from chapter 3 in Genesis, the first book of the Old Testament to Malachi chapter 3, the last book of the Old Testament where it is written: *"Then suddenly the Lord you are seeking will come to his temple, the messenger of the covenant whom you desire will come, says the Lord Almighty."* (Malachi 3:1). There are over 300 references to the coming of Christ the Lord in the Old Testament, so when Paul through the Holy Spirit writes: " *The Gospel he <u>promised</u> beforehand through his prophets in the holy Scriptures regarding his Son,* (Romans 1: 2-3) God's promise was not an isolated or small event. Now fast forward to the Corinthian Church and equate the promise they made for a "generous gift" (2 Corinthians 9: 5). There's hardly a comparison, yet God allows it to have major status by using the same word in the text.

God made the promise of his Son in the gospel, and then he gave fulfilling his promise. Things were never the same. That's the way it can be with you, your church and the world that you live in today even as it changed the Corinthian Church. They promised, they gave and they changed their life, the life of their church, and the world in which they lived. What an awesome concept! Understand then how you can put all this to use; put your faith in action by giving, saying and promising God the fulfillment of your pledge whatever it may be that you know is in God's will.

# CHAPTER 14

# Principles to Learn

Paul wanted the Corinthians to discover the principle for themselves so he reminded them that reaping is directly proportional to sowing. Furthermore, God looks at the heart of the giver and he reminds us that our motive and attitude are important. Don't give if you feel you are under compulsion or if you are reluctant, but give cheerfully for the apostle declares, *"God loves a cheerful giver"* (2 Corinthians 9:7). The Greek word for cheerful is "hilaros" from which we get the word – hilarious. What a great word picture this term presents! Later I will discuss becoming a hilarious giver: laugh your way to the eternal bank.

There are three reasons the apostle wants the Church to discover the principle. First, *"God is able to make all grace abound to you so that in all things, at all times having all that you need; you will abound in every good work."* (2 Corinthians. 9:8) God makes it happen! God, the owner, makes all grace abound to you at all times and you will abound in the work that he is doing. Talk about the difference between equity and debt! Well here it is: He allows you to be an equity shareholder in the work he is doing, and he does it through his abounding grace. Not only does he give you equity, he makes it abound, he makes you a large stockholder. The same thought is carried over in the next two verses when he says, *"He has scattered abroad his gifts to the poor, his righteousness endures forever"* (2 Corinthians 9:9). It is God who gives back. He is the one who is doing the scattering and he is using you to do it. The same thought continues in the next verse *"Now he who supplies seed to the sower and bread for food will also supply and increase your store of seed and will enlarge the harvest of your righteousness."* (2 Corinthians 9:10).

The second reason is Paul wants the Corinthians to discover the principle: God will *"supply and increase your store of seed and enlarge the harvest of your righteousness."* As a result of the giving God supplies, he increases, and he enlarges. When you put all three together, what you have is God, the subject of the sentence, strongly asserts that he will do this and that you should have intense anticipation on when he will cause this reality to come to pass. In case you still don't get it, he speaks plainly in verse 11 and says *"you will be made rich in every way so that you can be generous on every occasion and through us your generosity will result in thanksgiving to God."* There is the third reason Paul wants the Corinthians to discover the principle.

He wants them to be made materially rich so they can be generous, that they can be generous on every occasion. And now Paul hints at the blockbuster to come by saying that through them there is going to be a lot of thanks given as a result of their generosity. I believe what he is saying is this; your gift is going to have a huge impact and a lot of people are going to be affected. He further expands this thought when he says in verse 12 of 2 Corinthians 9, *"This service that you perform is not only supplying the needs of God's people, but is also overflowing in many expressions of thanks to God.* The word used for "many expressions of thanks" means many will be grateful because of this gift; not just God's people right now, but many people are going to come to Christ because of your generosity *"by which you have proved yourselves."*

In addition to a hunger for the Word of God, there are many evidences of spiritual rebirth in the life of new Christians. Their life seems different as "all things become new". One of the tangible signs that a person has become a Christian is he has a desire to give to the cause of Christ. Covetousness gives way to generosity; selfishness gives way to liberality. It's not "he who has the most toys wins" but he who has given his toys away wins later. Paul says, *"You have proved yourselves in this matter"* (2 Corinthians 9: 13). Furthermore, he writes, people *"are going to be grateful and praise God for the obedience that accompanies your confession of the gospel of Christ"*. Obedience is as multi-faceted as a diamond, and like an uncut diamond in the hand of the craftsman it starts to take shape as one surface is prepared and then another. As the diamond is cut and polished it takes shape and its beauty comes forth. One of the most difficult surfaces for us to become obedient in is, of course, giving. Consider this deep theological subject:

How difficult was the decision in the mind of God the Father to give his Son to be a propitiation for man's sin. And how difficult was the decision of the Son who is equal to God the Father to agree to that decision and allow himself to become the Sacrificial Lamb and to be slain for the expiation of sin. Who can plumb the depths of God's love and his grace? We read Christ humbled himself and was obedient unto death (Phil.2:8).

It is that kind of obedience we are called to in the area of giving. It puts a different light on the subject of sacrificial giving. And yet it is an obedience God rewards with spiritual as well as temporal blessings. Paul tells the Church that people are going to be grateful to them for doing this and hearts will go out to them because of the surpassing grace God has given to them. People are going to come to Christ and they are going to know they came to Christ as a result of the gift they are giving *"through the grace God has given you."* It is God's method and thanks be to him "for his indescribable gift," Jesus Christ. Did this actually happen? Did many people come to Christ and then know it was because of the Corinthian gift that they came to Christ? Look at what happens and you decide.

Titus and the brothers obviously go to Corinth and make arrangements to liquidate the gifts in kind. The collection probably raised a lot of funds because Paul decides to take the gift to Jerusalem and have the brothers go along with him. You may recall that in I Corinthians 16: 3 Paul says, *"then when I arrive I will give letters of introduction to the men you approve and send them with your gift to Jerusalem.* Then he writes in the next verse *"If it seems advisable for me to go also, they will accompany me."* From what we read in Romans 15:25, 26 we know that Paul took the gifts to Jerusalem himself and was accompanied by those from the Corinthian church as well as the other brothers. Whether it was the size of the gift or the character of it we don't know, but it is unlikely that it was a small amount. (This would seem to be the case from the description in 2 Corinthians 8:2 of the gift given by the Macedonians). It is likely, however, that the bulk of the funds came from the churches in Achaia of which Corinth would be prominent.

At any rate Paul took the gift to Jerusalem because he wanted to complete the task and make sure they received it in Jerusalem. If it had been a small sum of money it would not have been less important but it seems a larger amount would dictate care and control which would give no place to the appearance of impropriety of any sort. With the apostle Paul going along with the gift there would be no opportunity for such a scandal. Moreover the fact Paul was going along with the gift showed how important it was to the donors, how significant their gift in the eyes of the Lord that Paul would take a trip to Jerusalem himself. **That decision changed the course of history**!

## CHAPTER 15

# How History Was Changed

Instead of visiting Rome, which was his original plan, Paul writes to the church there instead. While he does not declare that he is writing from Corinth, it would seem so since Paul is writing from Gaius's house and as a result of this fact combined with the other references, most commentators agree that's the case. Regardless of the point of origin of the letter, the key point is that Paul wrote to the church at Rome instead of going there as originally planned because of the gift. (Romans 15:25-29) The letter then is used by God to change the world! How, you may ask, did he do that? Answer— God used the letter to the church at Rome in the conversion of many of the great saints of God, who in turn influenced changes in the course of history. Let's consider but a few of these significant conversions and the impact they had.

First of all there was the impact on the Church of Rome itself. The epistle contains the most complete explanation of the gospel and didactic systematic theology that may be found anywhere in Scripture. One can only imagine that it was like an atomic bomb dropped on the city. Because of the many greetings offered to the saints in Chapter 16, there had to be a great clamoring for a copy of the letter, in spite of the fact that it is longer than usual. The letter would eventually propel Rome to the forefront of the Gentile church. While an innumerable number of people have had their lives changed as a result of reading this letter to the church at Rome, here are but a few of the many examples of men whose lives changed and how they in turn changed the world of their day and the legacy of the change today.

One of the most notable of such was the great Augustine who has been called the greatest Latin Father of the early church. Born on a small farm in Algeria, he migrated to Rome and then to Milan where at the age of thirty two in the year 386AD he came under the conviction of God's Spirit because of what he says were his sexual passions. As the focus of his mother's prayers and Bishop Ambrose's preaching, Augustine later wrote in his <u>Confessions</u> "The tumult of my heart took me out into the garden where no one could interfere with the burning struggle with myself in which I was engaged, twisting and turning in my chains. I threw myself down somehow under a certain fig tree, and let my tears flow freely." Augustine knew in his soul he was in deep trouble spiritually and he hated it. He wrote: "Suddenly I heard a voice from the nearby house chanting as if it might be a boy or girl saying and repeating over and over again...Pick up and read, pick up and read...I interpreted it solely as a divine command to me to open the book and read the first chapter I might find...So I hurried back to the place where I had put down the book of the Apostle when I got up. I seized it, opened it, and in silence read the first passage on which my eye hit: "Not in riots and drunken parties, not in eroticism and indecencies, not in strife and rivalry, but put on the Lord Jesus Christ and make no provision for the flesh in its lusts." Augustine writes, "I neither wished nor needed to read further. At once with the last words of this sentence, it was as if a light of relief from all anxiety flooded into my heart. All the shadows of doubt were dispelled."[10]

Aurelius Augustinus, professor of literature and rhetoric, was transformed as God opened his spiritual eyes and he "put on the Lord Jesus Christ" and the robe of his Righteousness. We now refer to him as St. Augustine of Hippo, whose writings changed the world around him and had a lasting impact to this very day.

It was in an Augustinian cloister at Erfuhrt that another professor was ordained a monk and adopted Austeritzer (a lifestyle) as a method of obtaining salvation. The general consensus of thinking was it was the surest way to heaven and Martin Luther thought it's what he desired the most. He later would write, "If ever a monk got to heaven by his monkery, it was I." At Wittenberg University he taught on the letter to the church at Rome (1515-1516) and in the course of his classes came across the word in Greek "dikaiosyne" which may be translated just, righteous, upright. In verse 17 of chapter 1 of Romans it says, "For in the gospel a righteousness from God is revealed, a righteousness that is by faith from first to last, just as it is written: the righteous will live by faith." Luther was quite disturbed by the verse, as he understood it to mean God's righteousness was fulfilled by righteously punishing the unrighteous. Luther would later write "Night and day I pondered until I grasped the truth, that the righteousness of God, is that righteousness whereby through grace and sheer mercy, he justified us by faith. Thereupon I felt myself to be reborn and to have gone through open doors into paradise. The whole of Scripture took on a new meaning and whereas before the righteousness of God had filled me with hate, now it became to me inexpressibly sweet in greater love. This passage of Paul became to me, a gateway to heaven."[11]

Having come to an understanding of justification by faith at the age of thirty-eight, I can relate to feeling what Luther must have felt. I can only describe it as one of ecstatic joy. It occurred when someone sat in my living room and shared the good news of Christ using an illustration called "the record book of sin" with my wife and me. Suddenly, we grasped the principle concept of what Christ had done on the cross for us—more specifically—for me. It was as though someone had flipped on a light in a dark room. Things were never the same; afterwards all things became new. As I reflected on that day of salvation for me, I wrote this Poem. It is my hope the reader will indulge me in this bit of revelry.

It's a grand old story, how faith turns to glory
Sin's scarlet stains' washed whiter than snow
My spirit's set free for he's chosen me
That his grace and great love I may know

That his grace and great love I may show.

Free from my guilt and free from my shame
I'm freed to serve him and glorify his Name
There's healing and hope and peace in his way
And life's not the same since I met him that day
And life's not the same since he came to stay

Augustine and Luther were not the only famous conversions, that would come from the Book of Romans. You may recall John Wesley's famous entry in his journal, that was written on May 24, 1738 following a Moravian meeting in Aldersgate Street, London. Wesley after listening to someone read Luther's preface to the book of Romans wrote, "About a quarter before nine, while he was describing the changes which God works in the heart through faith in Christ, I felt my heart strangely warmed. I felt I did trust in Christ, Christ alone for salvation; an assurance was given me that he had taken away *my* sins, even mine, and saved me from the law of sin and death."[12]

Wesley had not been a Christian up until that time and while he had gone to the meeting that night, as we say kicking and screaming, he gained the assurance of eternal life. Earlier in 1735 Wesley and his brother had sailed to Georgia to serve as chaplains to the settlers and missionaries to the Indians. Returning to England two years later, the ship they were on ran into a big storm and they began to fear for their lives. The Moravians on board had a different view however. Singing away they proclaimed, "If this ship goes down, we go up." Confident in their Savior, the Moravians displayed a courage borne of their conviction. Such courage viewed by a non-believer under conviction of sin can be incomprehensible because they don't have God's grace to understand it. There is no warrior as brave as one who does not hold on to his life as something to be grasped!

Consider the greatest warrior of all, the Lord Jesus Christ, *"who being in very nature God, did not consider equality with God something to be grasped, but made himself nothing, taking the very nature of a servant, being made in human likeness, and being found in appearance as a man, he humbled himself and became obedient to death."*[13] The Moravians, warriors in their own right, did not fear death as John Wesley did at that time. "What could they know that I didn't, he reasoned. After all he had been the acknowledged leader of what was "The Holy Club" at Oxford University—a group formed to engage in sacred studies and other activities designed to earn eternal life by good works. Wesley would go forward into battle himself, founding the Methodist Church and having a great impact for the Kingdom of Christ. God used Paul's letter to the Romans in Wesley's life as only God could do it and he continued to use the letter as time unfolded.

Fast-forward to the early 1900's and you find God using it in the lives of Dimitru Cornilescu and Karl Barth, two contemporaries whose writings had a profound effect on the culture of their day. Using an analogy borne of the First World War, Roman Catholic theologian Karl Adam said Barth's commentary dropped "like a bombshell on the theologian's playground."[14] It was F.F. Bruce who drew attention to the fact that the use of the Book of Romans by

God in the lives of people was not limited to spiritual giants since "very ordinary men and women" have had their lives changed when they began to study this great letter. How much can we say about such men as John Calvin, Knox, Whitfield, all of whom had their lives impacted or transformed by the letter of Paul to the church at Rome, and they in turn had a huge impact on their culture, even to the point of changing the course of history and the world.

Would all of these changes have taken place in history without the use of Romans? Because it was the design of God to make such things happen, God never ordains an end without ordaining or providing the means to the end. In this case, the means was the faithfulness of the church at Corinth to a promise pledge. By keeping their promised pledge and having God bless their gift, it turned out to be "A GIFT THAT CHANGED THE WORLD." God obviously could have used any number of means to achieve his purpose, but it was his design to work it out this way. As Charles Hodge puts it, "all that occurs is due to the law of development or of self-manifestation of the Divine Being."[15] L. Berkhof puts it another way, "God and God only is the efficient cause of salvation, and in the distribution and communication of His grace, he is not absolutely bound to the divinely appointed means through which He ordinarily works, but uses them to serve His gracious purposes according to His own free will."[16] Berkhof further writes "God is a God of order, who in the operation of His grace ordinarily employs the means which He Himself has ordained. This of course does not mean that He has Himself becomes subservient to the appointed means and could not possibly work without them in the communication of His grace, but only that it has pleased Him to bind himself to the use of these means."[17]

Can you now see the tapestry of God's design in the gift promised by the Corinthians? It reminds me of when I was a young boy: My grandmother who was from Hungary and who had migrated to the United States made a lot of clothes for me. She didn't have any patterns to work from; she just had a design in mind. She would knit and knit and then she would call me over and hold up the material next to my growing body and she would make different comments to herself like "hmmm," "oh yea," "that needs it." Sometimes it would be an arm piece; another time it would be a square or an elongated piece of material. I never questioned her because I knew that she knew what she was doing. Oftentimes it made no sense to me that a particular piece she was holding up was part of what would become a beautiful sweater later. While it was a piece here and a piece there, in her mind she could already see the completed product on me even though it was far from finished.

And it wasn't just the clothes she made; it was the same for tablecloths, afghans and quilts. The point is the master craftsman can see the entire plan from beginning to end, knows how one piece fits with another and is pleased. My grandmother could see the finished product even before making it. The combination of design and God's faithfulness to his Word produces the product of grace that we put on and wear. It's called the righteousness of Christ and it's fitted unseen by us but complete and a perfect fit in the mind of the Father who chose in advance those who would wear it.

Is it still possible to change the world through your

giving or was the gift of the Corinthians a one-time situation God used and then put up on the shelf only to be used on special occasions—if they were ever to occur again? I submit that God is still in the business of changing lives, even nations to this date, as a result of faithful giving, particularly when it's above and beyond the tithe.

# CHAPTER 16

# Is Tithing Still Required In Today's Church?

A question that is often asked today is what is the tithe and how much should I give? Is it 10% of the gross I make or is it 10% of the net I take home after taxes? I was discussing this topic with a friend of mine recently and I was shocked to hear him say that he believed that it was 10% of the net after taxes. I think that was a topic in Christ's day also when the Pharisees tried to catch the Lord Jesus with words. "Tell us" they said "is it right to pay taxes to Caesar or not?"[18] The implications of the question were many. If the Lord said it was not right to pay taxes, the Pharisees could report Jesus to the Romans and say this man preaches and teaches that it is not right for the Jews to pay taxes. The Romans would view this as an insurrection and come and arrest Jesus, which is precisely what the Pharisees wanted. If, on the other hand, Jesus said it was right to pay taxes, the Jews would make him out to be a type of Publican—a fundraiser for the Romans and a supporter of Caesar and the Jews hated being under the rule of Rome.

Presuming an inescapable dilemma, the Pharisees tried to hang the Lord up on a two- prong answer of a no win situation. When the Lord asked them whose picture was on the coin, the Jews had to answer, Caesar's. The answer in turn hung the Jews up on a dilemma because if Caesar's picture was on it, it had to be Caesar's. The subsequent statement *"to render unto God the things that are God's"* did not have the qualifier "after you have given to Caesar" before it. Very simply, the Lord made no provision for the deduction of Caesar's portion out of God's portion, which is what would happen if a person tithed on the net instead of the gross amount of income.

Recently, I heard someone say, that the New Testament does not teach tithing and Jesus never taught tithing. Nothing can be farther from the truth! On the contrary, the Lord of the Old Testament is the Lord of the New Testament also, *"I the Lord do not change."* (Malachi 3: 6) The very chapter in Malachi where God says, " *Return unto me and I will return unto you."* (Malachi 3:7b) is preceded by the statement, *"God does not change."* If he did away with tithing in the New Testament he would have changed his mind, but it never happened, never will. *"Will a man rob God?"* (Malachi 3:8). The question is as applicable today as the day God asked it of Israel through the prophet Malachi. Like the nation of Israel the people of God, we the people of God today will ask the same, *"How did we rob you?"*

The notion that tithing is not required in the Church

today and that Jesus never taught tithing is rebutted in Matthew 23:23. The context is when Jesus is addressing the crowds. You may recall the question and answer time between the Pharisees and Jesus on the subject of taxes. The Sadducees had a question for him on the topic of the resurrection, and one expert in the law questioned him regarding the greatest commandment. Then Jesus asked a question of the Pharisees regarding the Christ, *"Whose son is he?"* When the Pharisee's answered, *"The son of David."* Jesus then points out that David called him Lord (Psalm.1: 10). *"If then David calls him Lord, how can he be his son?"* We read then *"No one could say a word in reply."* (Matthew 22:46) The point was not lost on the Pharisees; they knew the implication of the answer. The Messiah-Christ was God incarnate as the son of David. Jesus then addresses the hypocrisy of the Pharisees and pronounces seven woes that are found in Matthew 23. The specific woe in verse 23 is on the subject of tithing. *"Woe to you teachers of the law and Pharisees, you hypocrites! You give a tenth of your spices – mint, dill and cumin. But you have neglected the more important matters of the law, justice, mercy and faithfulness. You should have practiced the latter <u>without neglecting the former.</u>"* In other words,<u> you did what you were supposed to do when you tithed your herb garden's yield.</u>

Living in south Florida has a lot of advantages, one of which is being able to cultivate an outdoor herb garden in a large pot just outside the kitchen door. When my wife wants fresh parsley, all she has to do is open the door and cut what she needs from the big pot which seems to replace what she harvested earlier in a short period of time. What a difference the way food tastes with fresh herbs! We keep no record of the amount, type or time the herbs are cut. I cannot imagine keeping such records to make sure I don't miss tithing the portion used, but the Pharisees obviously did keep track. In fact they were so obsessed with keeping the Law, they were blind as to what were the really important matters of the Law. In other words you are suppose to tithe but don't become so focused on the small stuff, that you forget what is really important. As Jesus put it, *"You strain out a gnat but swallow a camel."* (Matthew 23:24) Tithing is important but not as important as the condition of your heart. The teaching of Jesus on the Sermon on the Mount is consistent with the principle: *"Therefore if you are offering your gift at the altar and there remember that your brother has something against you, leave your gift there at the front of the altar. First go and be reconciled to your brother, then come and offer your gift."* (Matthew 5: 23) The Macedonians got it right. You will recall Paul wrote, *"They gave themselves first to the Lord and then to us in keeping with God's will."* (2 Corinthians 8:5) The Macedonian hearts were right with the Lord and their desire to give followed.

The New Testament principle is that giving should be out of the abundance that God has provided. It's not really a new idea but is a principle that is grounded in the "first fruits" concept. *"Honor the Lord with thy substance and with the first fruits of all thine increase so shalt thy barns be filled with plenty and thy presses shall burst out with new wine."*(Proverbs 3:9 KJV) The key word I point to is all in the increase. Once again, there is no provision for the deduction or the exclusion for taxes or other slices off the top. There are no overrides to be deducted before God gets His share. Another question, that may be asked in today's environment of multiple ministries competing for the same dollar is: "What is the storehouse?" For the command of God in Malachi is: *"Bring the whole tithe into the storehouse"* (Malachi 3:10). It is not my desire to opine on this subject so I will just say that I believe it's the local church where the believer attends.

# CHAPTER 17

# Can We Change The World We Live In Today?

So the question remains, is it still possible to change the world through your giving today? Dr. D. James Kennedy is the primary speaker on the radio program "Truths that Transform" and I remember him saying on the program one day, "You can change the world." I remember thinking at the time, that's pretty bold, but I knew what he was saying. God can use <u>you</u> to make a difference when he changes the world. Is God changing the world now?

Have you ever heard of Evangelism Explosion III International, or as it is referred to simply as EE? In the year 2002, EE under the title of "Heart to Heart" conducted 150 Leadership Clinics in what was the former Soviet Union. Not many years ago it was considered a criminal offense to preach Jesus Christ there and many were locked up for doing it, for at that time the Soviet Union was officially atheistic. Because "explosion" is still a dangerous word, the name of the Ministry was changed to "Heart to Heart" but the methodology, content and principles of EE remain unchanged and God is using it to change the world of the former Soviet Union. Top Communist party members, as well as the ordinary citizens of the Soviet Union are coming to know Christ throughout the birthplace of Communism. Praise God! Over one thousand pastors and key leaders will be trained on how to train others, who will in turn train others how to share Christ in an intelligent manner, using on the job training. They are having an enormous impact in those countries. God is changing the world of the former Soviet Union. How did it start-what happened?

A missionary team from EE entered the country and the Spirit of God moved upon the people. At first there were a few, then more, then a lot more started coming to Christ. Now they are coming by the thousands and soon it will be by the ten thousands and then hundreds of thousands and millions as the Spirit of God moves across that vast country. Question: Who paid the missionary teams expenses for them to travel to the former Soviet Union? Without the funds to make the journey, the team stays home. Who paid the organizations expenses to operate the ministry, the rent, telephone, electric, equipment and salaries? Who provided the missionary team's food and clothing, pencils, pens and paper clips? Who provided funds to operate the church where the missionary team was fed and nurtured? Did the donors who provided the funds know they were going to change the world? Do you think even one of them said,"I am going to give this gift and change the world with it"? Of course not!

The Corinthians didn't know they were going to change the world either, yet God makes it clear in 2 Corinthians 9:9. The Apostle writes: *"He has scattered abroad his gifts to the poor, his righteousness endures for ever."* Once again, beginning in verse 12 of 2 Corinthians 9, *"This service that you perform is not only supplying the needs of God's people but is also overflowing in many expressions of thanks to God." "Men will praise God for your generosity in sharing with them and everyone else"* (2 Corinthians 9: 13). We cannot comprehend how grateful the people of the former Soviet Union and others throughout the world are today, but we can be sure of this fact; on judgment day we will know.

In the account of the judgment the Lord tells us that: *"he will separate the people one from another as a shepherd separates the sheep from the goats"* (Matthew 25:32), as God invites the blessed to *"take your inheritance"* (Matthew 25:34), there follows a discourse by God followed by a question from the people and an answer by God. What is striking about this scene is the way they were separated- givers from non-givers. For the Lord will say: " I was hungry and you gave me something to eat, you gave me something to drink, you gave me shelter, you gave me clothe, you gave me your personal time when I was sick and in prison." (Matthew 25:35-37). When the coin is flipped over and the other side is looked at God says: *"At no time did you feed me when I was hungry, at no time did you give me to drink when I was thirsty"* (Matthew 25:42-43). Givers versus non-givers, sheep and the goats, saved and the lost, these are the categories. Now I want to make it perfectly clear that I am not saying giving or any other form of works saves a person.

Salvation is by grace alone through faith alone in Christ alone; works have no part in justification. It is interesting, however, that one of the ways the Lord will separate the people of the earth is givers vs. non-givers. Of course the main distinction is the righteous from the unrighteous.

Do you want to be used of God to change the world? How to begin and how to keep going are the topics of the rest of this book. First, believe God can do it and take him at his Word. The Scripture says " *without faith it is impossible to please God, because anyone who comes to him must believe that he exists and that he rewards those who earnestly seek him"* (Heb 11:6) Again in Hebrews the writer says, *"So do not throw away your confidence, it will be richly rewarded"* (Hebrews 10:35). Believing God is there and that he wants to demonstrate his love through you is the launch point not only for giving but also for a life of service in gratitude for what he has done for you. Furthermore, the writer of Hebrews tells us that God will reward confidence when he comes. One can only speculate what that reward may be, but know this for sure: if you don't receive it you will wish for all eternity that you did receive it.

Rewards should not be the reason for giving or for that matter neither should good works be done for rewards. All good works should be done out of gratitude for what God through his Son Jesus Christ has done for us. It is, however, as if God says I am watching and I see what you are doing. John writes and quotes him *"that is the First and the Last"* saying *"I know you, your deeds, your love and your faith, your service and perseverance and that you are now doing more than you did at first"* (Rev 2:19). So if believing in

God is the launch point, the reaction is repentance and the motivator is the Holy Spirit.

Confession of your short-comings in the area of giving and the establishment of a mindset that you want God to use you and that you will be faithful in the area of personal finance and giving, will clear the air so to speak. God's promise is that "*if we confess our sins, he is faithful and just to forgive us and cleanse us from all unrighteousness*" (I John 1:9). The sin of not being faithful with our finances is, of course, a sin of omission and commission—omission because we didn't give, but also commission because we robbed God by doing it. (Mat 3:8) Finally, ask God to fill you with his Holy Spirit.

Apart from God's Spirit working in our lives, giving of our time, talent and especially treasure will seem like a very foolish thing to do, especially by those who don't know Christ as Savior. Like any good work done for the cause of Christ, giving comes from a heart filled with the joy of salvation; a joy that may be described as hilarity and flows from the absolute assurance of salvation and an attitude of "who cares about this, I have the riches of Heaven awaiting me." Having prepared yourself to give let the fun begin.

# CHAPTER 18

# Becoming A Hilarious Giver

The way to begin is by taking a long hard look at stuff, i.e. possessions. Over time we tend to accumulate "stuff" that we don't use or for that matter won't use in the future. This is particularly true in the area of clothes. Styles change along with our waistlines and over time we fill our dresser drawers and closets with "stuff" we would not be caught dead wearing. So start in your closets and decide to give away everything that you haven't worn for the last year, and won't be wearing in the next year. The key here is to be ruthless and at the same time generous. If you use a pragmatic approach and tend to rationalize saying "I may need this or that" when deep down you know the chances of you wearing the item are slim to none, send it to the thrift store. In fact, adopt this as your motto—if in doubt, throw it out. (thrift store) (Seems I've heard that before).

"Stuff" can be something we cling to or give up and ask God to use for his glory.

After Hurricane Andrew struck South Florida, the area looked like a large bomb had hit it. Overhead pictures from aircraft showed the magnitude of the disaster. It was interesting to note people's reaction to having what amounted to all of their earthly possessions stripped away from them or removed so they could not get to them. The National Guard was called in to prevent looting and the local media covering the disaster often included an interview with the local residents of the area. One could not help but notice and contrast two different attitudes of the people.

One group seemed to be utterly devastated. The news cameras would pan a resident and then show a pile of debris that used to be his house. The resident would inevitably be crying and his message would be something like "I don't know what I'm going to do now; all my "stuff" was in that house. Now I'm sure it is a very traumatic thing to lose your house and all your possessions in one day and I am not making light of it. A certain amount of remorse is to be expected as all the lifetime memories you have in a house are suddenly blown away to who knows where. But the reaction of the individuals who lost their "stuff " is what I focused on in the reports. Contrasted against group one's reaction was a second group who had a different world and life view.

Perhaps the latter group epitomized by Collins and Shirley who were out of town when the storm hit their house and neighborhood. The storm surge brought a wave of water and combined with sustained category four winds, clobbered their house in Kendall. When Collins and Shirley returned home all their "stuff" was in a heap, very little was salvageable. Yet when talking with them later, Collins had a smile on his face as he described his "stuff" and what was left of it. Far from being devastated by their loss, they viewed the loss as God's will for them and while a lot of earthly possessions were removed, they knew they had a lot better "stuff" waiting for them in eternity. They knew that *"no eye has seen, no ear has heard, no mind has conceived what God has prepared for those who love him"*. (1 Corinthians 2:9).

Collins and Shirley's group two reactions demonstrated an eternal prospective for "stuff" that God gives us. While God places it in our hand, it's how we hold it that's important. Do you grip it tightly or do you hold it with an open hand? Are you a giver or do you withhold? Remember the final judgment discourse between God and the people of the earth, "I was naked and you clothed me." Ask God to use the clothes you give away to clothe his people.

There is a day in Canada known as "boxing day". Before I knew what the day was celebrating, I used to think it was a day devoted to the sport of boxing; after all there is a great deal of interest in the sport in Canada. Actually, the day has nothing to do with the sport of boxing, but it is a day which is devoted to "boxing up" all of the possessions a person has which the person is willing to give away to someone else who could use it. What a great holiday! We could use a day like that here in the United States whereas the average household here has more excess than any place else in the world.

While we may not have a day devoted to the concept

here in the U.S., it certainly is something that we as individual families could profit from doing as well as our church family. If this sounds like something you would like to do as a church family, go ask your Pastor if your church could celebrate a "Boxing Day." The movement may just spread throughout your church and your denomination. Can you imagine what it would be like to have a worldwide "boxing day"? In a sense, the church at Corinth had a time when they "boxed up" their "stuff" and gave it to God in the form of gifts in kind.

# CHAPTER 19

# Gifts In Kind –
# Developmental Giving

Before we begin to talk about gifts in kind that can be made under existing tax law here in the United States, the subject of excessive personal debt needs to be addressed. One might ask, "How could I begin to tithe and give above the tithe when I don't have enough money because of personal debt that I have incurred? Personal debt of individuals in the U.S. is at an all time historical high as I write. It is the amount of debt versus the amount of income a person has which will determine the course of action necessary to get out of debt. If it is a large amount of personal debt, there are personal credit counseling agencies, which are available to help you. Generally speaking, a credit agency will negotiate with creditors for you, in order to resolve the pressure of being hounded by collection people.

The idea is to structure some kind of payment plan

whereby income can be matched against expenses and payments made to creditors on a regular basis until the debt is paid in its entirety. The process requires personal discipline on the part of the debtor. There will be times during the repayment period where it will be easy to "fall off the wagon" and buy something that you think you must have in order to survive. Success in getting out of debt is not only paying off what you owe in timely payments, but also by cutting off new debt sources such as your credit cards and haunts where you spend—such as the mall.

The personal discipline to get out of debt usually requires a lifestyle change and a change of heart. The way to begin then is by asking God to help you start over again. Confess that your sinful lifestyle has been a violation of the Tenth Commandment and repent. Ask God to help you get out of the mess you are in so you can be faithful and generous in your lifestyle, and mean it. Claim God's promise in Proverbs, which declares, *"Trust in the Lord with all your heart and lean not on your own understanding, in all your ways acknowledge him, and he shall make your paths straight"* (Proverbs 3:5-6).

Personal debt is a homeboy of obesity and it is just as hard to overcome because it is a matter of the will. Staying out of high personal debt is a lot like keeping the fat off after you lose weight and God can help you do both.

But suppose personal debt is not a problem for you; God has blessed you with personal wealth and you would like to do more, but you just don't know how to begin to use some of the assets you have acquired. In the remaining pages of this chapter, a couple of different ways of giving a gift in kind will be discussed, the kind of gifts that can change the world. The strategies presented do not propose to offer tax advice or legal advice, and before a person enters into any of the transfers presented, the donor should consult his or her professional tax advisor.


## Transfer #1

## Charitable Gift Annuity


Like its namesake, the gift annuity has two components: the gift portion and the annuity portion. It is one of the best transfers a person getting on in age can make. The reason is the annuity payment is a factor of a donor's age. Very simply, the older a person is , the higher the percentage rate, which may be paid on a gift annuity, because the number of years of payout is less. The prevailing interest rate at the time the gift annuity is completed is also a factor. The calculations may be based on one or two lives. The prevailing rate of interest paid on the annuity portion is generally the same at most qualified charities that are members of the Committee on Gift Annuities. The Committee is a service organization that assists qualified charities in administration of the overall program of issuing annuities.

Many states regulate the issuance of gift annuities through the State Department of Insurance or its equivalent. In a time period of low interest rates throughout the country, the gift annuity becomes attractive for a portion of available investment funds. The gift annuity transfer is irrevocable; so once the transfer of assets or purchase of a gift annuity is completed, one can't ask for the money to be returned, unlike a CD or a deferred annuity purchased from a commercial insurance company. Here is how the gift annuity works.

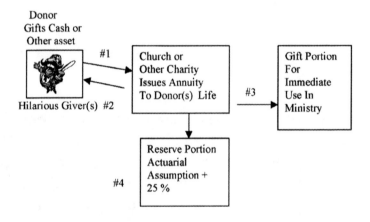

#1. Donor gifts—cash (transfers property to the charity); or any other asset of value that can be liquidated, and used to purchase an annuity, which will be issued by the charity to the donor. Not just cash, but any asset which can be liquidated for cash, whether it is appreciated in value or not. Generally speaking, the asset gifted should be owned free and clear, i.e., no mortgages or liens.

#2. The charity in turn gives back to the donor a certificate of annuity, which is a promise to pay a specified, agreed upon sum of money. This sum of money is agreed upon prior to the gift being made to charity.

#3. The charity in turn, gets to use some of the money as a gift right away, to use as they see fit, as allowed by the IRS code, and the stated purpose of the donee.

#4. The rest of the money is escrowed by the charity in an escrow fund designated as such and segregated from the rest of the charity's general funds. The amount of money segregated is determined by the actuarial tables, which estimate how long a person will live. That is to say statistical studies show that if you put a large group of people of the same age into a pool, some people will die early, some will live longer and there will be a mean (average) determined. Take that mean age, and then add a 25% cushion and that is the number the charity should escrow. I don't know of any issuer of gift annuities who is a member of the Committee on Gift Annuities who doesn't do it this way.

The gift portion as illustrated in (3) generates a tax deduction, which may be used to offset income tax due on the donor's individual tax return. The impact of the deduction on a 1040 tax return will vary based on an individual's tax bracket. Another tax consideration is: A portion of the income stream paid to the donor will have an exclusion ratio based upon a number of factors which are determined in the IRS annuity tables. That is to say, a portion of the income stream will be tax-free because it represents a return of your own principal on which you have already paid tax.

In the event a prospective donor wants to make a gift but the donee-charity does not issue gift annuities, the donor may contact me, c/o Box 40, Fort Lauderdale, FL 33300.

## Transfer #2

## The Charitable Remainder Trust

The Charitable Remainder Trust has two different modes: the Unitrust and the Annuity Trust. While similar, each is distinctly different from the other and is distinguished by the way it pays out to the income beneficiary. The Charitable Remainder Unitrust pays out a fixed percentage of the assets in the trust and the annuity trust pays out a fixed sum of money from the Trust. The Charitable Reminder trust, referred to as a "CRT", is the centerpiece of my favorite transfer. While it may seem complex when you first look at it, I assure you it is all based on existing IRS code and is quite legal. I say that because after I show it to people and they grasp the advantages and tax treatment, usually the first thing a client will say "Is that legal?" Are you sure I can do that without getting in trouble with the IRS?"

I am often asked, "What is a trust?" The answer is it's a document which creates an entity similar to a corporation inasmuch as it finds its standing under the current law that was handed down to us from old English Law that serves as a foundation for law in America today. The entity has a tax identification number and must file a tax return every year. There are three parties to any trust: The settler or grantor, the trustee, and the beneficiary or beneficiaries. The terms settler or grantor refer to the same person or persons. It is the title given to the creator of a trust, the one who establishes it, or sets it up. The trustee is the party that administers and takes possession of the property or assets of the trust. The third party to the trust is the beneficiary or beneficiaries of the trust. The trust beneficiary receives the property in the trust at the appointed time of distribution. A financial advisor may provide tax and financial advice on setting up a trust, but because a trust is a legal document, it should be drafted by an attorney licensed to practice law in the State where it is created and executed.

The transfer begins by having the donor or donors create two irrevocable trusts, a CRT and a life insurance trust, which I call a wealth replacement trust, sometimes referred to as an ILIT (Irrevocable Life Insurance Trust). The advantage of the ILIT is the donor can still have the children or other heirs receive the same amount of the value of the asset that was given away through the charitable trust.

The transfer gift, in this illustration is any asset. An asset that is highly appreciated has a low cost basis and a low current yield or cash flow is the ideal candidate. A classic example would be a piece of land appreciated in price, but with no cash flow or income. Other assets, such as stocks, buildings, or share of a private company do just as well. Here is how it works.

**Transfer #2**
**CHARITABLE REMINDER TRUST**

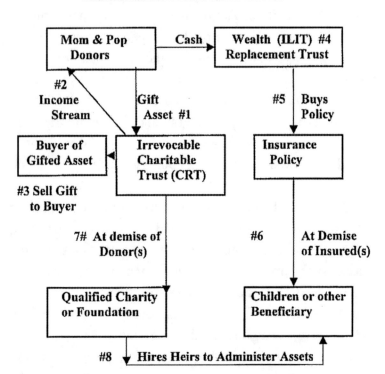

(#1) Mom and/or Pop Donor decide to gift an appreciated asset to be used by God after their demise. After consulting their tax advisor, they set up an irrevocable Charitable Remainder Trust (CRT) and other entities illustrated on the page. The term "irrevocable" describes the trust, because once the gift is transferred to the trust, it is complete and cannot be reversed. Nevertheless, having made the decision to gift the asset, the transfer is made to the CRT.

(#2) In turn, the CRT gives a note to the donors, which guarantees the donor an income for life. The income is either a percentage of the asset value of the trust on a specified date or a fixed amount in regular specified payments to begin immediately, or a set date in the future. The trust must comply with current tax law, which dictates a certain percentage of the initial value of the CRT must go to the charitable beneficiary (currently 10% in 2004) in order to receive a deduction on the donor's tax return. The deduction the donor receives is an amount that is deductible in the year of the gift with a five-year carry-forward of the unused portion of the deduction. The deduction is available to be used against the donors adjusted gross income with a limitation of 50 percent (of AGI) in any one year.

(#3.) The charitable trust sells the asset, which was gifted to it, to obtain funds to make the note payments to the donor. In the event the cash flow is sufficient to cover the payments, the trustee, who is independent, may decide to retain the asset, after consulting with the donor on the relative merits of the sale. Certain assets, such as vacant land, may need an appraisal to validate the tax deduction. The tax deduction, along with the increased cast flow from the low yield gifted asset, comes into play with the next step of replacing the value of the asset which was gifted.

(#4.) A Wealth Replacement Trust (ILIT) is another irrevocable trust in which the independent trustee administers the assets in the trust. The object of the trust is to convey the assets in the trust to the beneficiary of the trust—free from estate taxes. There are a couple of mistakes to avoid, but having avoided them, the donor can use the money saved on taxes and the increased cash flow to purchase a life insurance policy on the life of the donor, or joint with a spouse.

(#5.) At the demise of the insured, the insurance contract pays the trust the value of the policy, which may be the approximate value of the asset gifted to the CRT. Thus the name: Wealth Replacement Trust. The premiums for the policy can be gifted to the ILIT tax free at the rate of $11,500 per donor per donee per year (2004). That is to say, a husband and wife may gift $23,000 jointly to as many individual beneficiaries as the trust has. For example, with two children who are beneficiaries, the husband and wife can gift $46,000 tax free to the ILIT, using a provision known as the "Crummy Letter" provision. Premium payments must be made on the policy five of the first seven years of the contract. With proper planning, the entire amount will pass tax-free.

(#6.) Concurrent with the demise of the last income beneficiary, the Charity receives the corpus of the trust (whatever is in there), which may be more or less than the original gift.

(#7.) Of course, it too passes tax free, but it is not over yet. A wrinkle I have added to this plan is the beneficiary of the CRT is a public foundation (509)(A)(1) status under the IRS Code and, unlike a private foundation, it is eligible to receive gifts for 501(C)(3) work, i.e., religious, educational, public works.

(#8.) Instead of having to distribute a portion of the trust and all its income, like a private foundation, the public foundation trustees may choose the when and where of gift distribution. Furthermore, the foundation may hire advisors to determine qualified recipients of distributions. There is no reason why the children of the donor of the CRT asset can't be hired to provide such advice to the foundation (#8) provided the foundation trustee will hire them.

This transfer should be done only in the context of an estate plan designed to achieve the needs, goals, and objectives of an individual and should only be completed through the advice of a planning team which would include a tax advisor, insurance agent, and an attorney qualified to draft legal documents and render tax-planning advice. An individual planning such a transfer and unable to find competent advisors may contact this author at Box 40, Fort Lauderdale FL 33308.

# Conclusion

God's Spirit is moving throughout the world today just as he has throughout history. More people are coming to Christ in places we never dreamed of before – such as the example we discussed in the former Soviet Union. Another hot spot is China. Who would have believed that China would be quickened by the millions, yet its happening today and given the current exponential rate of growth, China will become a Christian nation in the future. Case in point, South Korea and what has taken place there. Finally look at the revival that is occurring in the United States. All we have to do is look at the number of Christian legislators elected now versus sixteen years ago. All of which leads me to believe that we are in the end of the end times. Christ is the Centerpiece of God in history.

You have God's invitation to have a share in the work he is doing, as we discussed. One of the best ways to have an immediate impact is to identify a ministry that God is using throughout the world and send it a monthly support check. It is not unlike buying shares of stock in a company that is growing and has potential to produce big profits.

I often ask stockbrokers and people who invest in the stock market " what determines where the price of a stock will trade?' I am amazed at some of the answers I get from people. Some of the more common answers are "more buyers than sellers", or price earnings ratios of the industry. Some give a technical answer based on the balance sheet and income statement! I will give you my answer, that I know to be correct, although I have never read it anywhere, as stated: "The company's ability to earn and investor sentiment regarding those earnings." While it is not my desire to expound on the stock market, I can tell you if you want to invest for a profit, the next time your broker suggests a stock to purchase, ask him or her, what did the company earn per share for the last two years and what are its estimates per share for the next three years? If the answers don't roll of the brokers tongue, run the other way. The principle of investing in ministry is not dissimilar.

Research the work of the ministry and check out the fruit of its efforts. What results has it been blessed with for the last two or three years, i.e., what is God doing through its ministry? How is it impacting the cause of Christ and what is the estimate of the ministry's harvest for the next three years. What is the ministry's "earnings per share," which is to say, "How much did it cost to produce the results"? Did most of the operational expenses go toward overhead, or were the results exceptional for the ministry's budget?

Perhaps the most effective and fruitful ministry that

does more (earnings) for winning souls for Christ than any other work or ministry today is Evangelism Explosion International, or as its known simply as "EE". With the world famous two diagnostic questions, EE does more for the cause of Christ on the lowest operating budget than any other major ministry I know of today. The reason is simple; it uses unpaid laymen to bring people to Christ through one-on- one personal witnessing. The ministry trains laymen to train others who in turn train others how to share the good news of salvation. When those who are trained train others the multiplication factor kicks in and provides exponential growth. It's a low budget platform that is now operational in every nation and continent in the world, its growth has been phenomenal. Investing in EE is like supporting a missionary team in the first century. Remember the missionary team that went into the Soviet Union and had good results; they were (are) with EE, (a/k/a Heart to Heart).

Another good investment is in the theological education of future preachers of the gospel. In a time when a lot of seminaries have gone liberal in their theological views, even to the point of denying the deity of Christ and the inerrancy of the Bible, there are several that remain solid in doctrine and preparation for ministry. Knox Theological Seminary in Ft. Lauderdale, Florida is at, or tied for the top of the list. Consider this question – how would you have liked to have been an investor / supporter of the Apostle Paul. You can be an underwriter of a great future pastor by investing in such a place as Knox Theological Seminary.

Here's a fun thing to do: Identify a missionary who is working on a mission field that interests you and partner with him. Find out how you can support his work with your time, talent, and treasure. Enter into a prayer covenant with him and delegate resources to him; hold him accountable, ask him for reports. If you're not satisfied with his performance replace him and find another partner. Your church missions committee and your denomination's missionary list are a great way to prospect for your partners.

Hearing what God is doing in other parts of the world (by using the missionary you support) will stretch your vision for the world and give you a desire to increase your gifts as God gives the harvest.

Ask God to use your gift in the work he is doing – ask him to use it to change the world. May God bless you and keep you – Amen.

# Notes

[1] Kennon Callahan, <u>Giving and Stewardship In An Effective Church</u>. (San Francisco: Josey- Bass Publishers, 1992). p. 49.

[2] Callahan, p. 50.

[3] loc.cit.

[4] sup.

[5] Ron Blue, <u>Generous Living</u>. (Michigan: Zondervan Publishing House. 1977) p. 99

[6] Blue, p. 101

[7] Phillip E Hughes. <u>The Second Epistle To The Corinthians</u>. (Michigan: Eerdmans Publishing Co. 1979). p. 290

[8] Alfred Edersheim, <u>The Life And Times Of Jesus The Messiah</u>. (Michigan: Eerdmans Publishing Co. 1977) ,op.cit. 566 rpt. (Oxford 1886)

[9] Edersheim, The Life And Times Of Jesus The Messiah. P.566

[10] Augustine, Confessions <u>Book V111</u>, pp 146-153

[11] John Stott's Commentary On Romans, <u>God's Good News To The World</u> indicates this is FF Bruce's free translation of Luther's own

account.

[12] John Wesley's Journal, from the entry May 24,1738.

[13] Philippians Chapter 2: 6-8

[14] Quoted by Bruce,. , and Stott. N.D.

[15] Charles Hodge, <u>Systematic Theology,Vol. 1</u>, (Michigan: Eerdmans Publishing Co. 1979,) p. 539

[16] L. Berkhof. <u>Systematic</u> Theology . 4th Edition, ( Eerdmans. 1977). p539

[17] Ibid.

[18] Ibid

# A Selected Bibliography

The Bible. <u>The Hebrew-Greek Key Study Bible</u>, New International Version. Chattanooga, Tennessee. AMG Publishers. 1996.

Augustinus, Saint Aurelius. <u>Confessions Book Vlll</u>

Berkhof, L. <u>Systematic Theology</u> 4<sup>th</sup> Edition. Michigan: Eerdmans. 1977.

Blue, Ron with Jodie Berndt. <u>Generous Living</u> Michigan: Zondervan Publishing House. 1997

Callahan, Kennon L. <u>Giving And Stewardship In An Effective Church</u>. San Francisco: Josey-Bass Publishers. 1992.

Edersheim, Alfred. The Life And Times Of Jesus The Messiah Michigan: Eerdmans. 1977

Hodge, Charles. Systematic Theology 4th Edition. Michigan: Eerdmans. 1979

Hughes, Phillip E. The Second Epistle To the Corinthians. Michigan: Eerdmans. 1979

Stott, John. Commentary On Romans-God's Good News To The World Illinois: Inter Varsity Press. 1968

Wesley, John. Wesley's Journal Entry May 24, 1738